The Math Experiment

Why this book?	9
The experiment and organization of the book	14
Week 0 – Getting started with the Math Club	17
Week 1	20
Week 1 Letter to the Parents	20
Week 1 Story – Apollo 13	20
Week 1 Curriculum – More or Less	23
Level 1	24
Level 2	25
Level 3	27
Week 1 Three Little Birds	29
Week 1 Angry Bird	30
Week 2	31
Week 2 Letter to the Parents	31
Week 2 Story – The Number of Days in Each Month	31
Week 2 Curriculum – Dates and Times	33
Level 1	33
Level 2	34
Level 3	35
Week 2 Three Little Birds	37
Week 2 Angry Bird	38
Week 3	39
Week 3 Letter to the Parents	39
Week 3 Story – Fibonacci Numbers	40
Week 3 Curriculum – Patterns	42
Level 1	42
Level 2	43
Level 3	44
Week 3 Three Little Birds	46
Week 3 Angry Bird	46
Week 4	47
Week 4 Letter to the Parents	47

- Week 4 Story – Terence Tao ... 48
- Week 4 Curriculum - Fractions ... 49
  - Level 1 ... 49
  - Level 2 ... 51
  - Level 3 ... 53
- Week 4 Three Little Birds ... 55
- Week 4 Angry Bird ... 55

Week 5 ... 56
- Week 5 Letter to the Parents ... 56
- Week 5 Story - Carl Friedrich Gauss ... 57
- Week 5 Curriculum – Ordered Lists ... 57
  - Level 1 ... 57
  - Level 2 ... 59
  - Level 3 ... 60
- Week 5 Three Little Birds ... 62
- Week 5 Angry Bird ... 62

Week 6 ... 63
- Week 6 Letter to the Parents ... 63
- Week 6 Story - Melanie Wood ... 63
- Week 6 Curriculum – Introduction to Multiplication ... 65
  - Level 1 ... 65
  - Level 2 ... 66
  - Level 3 ... 67
- Week 6 Three Little Birds ... 68
- Week 6 Angry Bird ... 69

Week 7 ... 70
- Week 7 Letter to the Parents ... 70
- Week 7 Story – The International Math Olympiad ... 70
- Week 7 Curriculum – Introduction to Division ... 72
  - Level 1 ... 72
  - Level 2 ... 73
  - Level 3 ... 74

- Week 7 Three Little Birds ... 75
- Week 7 Angry Bird ... 75
- Week 8 ... 76
  - Week 8 Letter to the Parents ... 76
  - Week 8 Story – Srinivasa Ramanujan ... 76
  - Week 8 Curriculum – Number Riddles ... 77
    - Level 1 ... 77
    - Level 2 ... 77
    - Level 3 ... 78
  - Week 8 Three Little Birds ... 79
  - Week 8 Angry Bird ... 79
- Math Competitions ... 80
  - Noetic Math Contest ... 80
  - Math Kangaroo ... 80
  - Continental Mathematics League ... 81
- Rock and Roll – More Practice Problems ... 82
- Final Note – The Results of the Experiment ... 85
- Solutions ... 86
  - Week 1 ... 86
    - Level 1 ... 86
    - Level 2 ... 89
    - Level 3 ... 94
    - Three Little Birds ... 102
    - Angry Bird ... 104
  - Week 2 ... 105
    - Level 1 ... 105
    - Level 2 ... 106
    - Level 3 ... 108
    - Three Little Birds ... 109
    - Angry Bird ... 111
  - Week 3 ... 111
    - Level 1 ... 111

- Level 2 112
- Level 3 113
- Three Little Birds 114
- Angry Bird 115

Week 4 115
- Level 1 115
- Level 2 117
- Level 3 120
- Three Little Birds 123
- Angry Bird 125

Week 5 126
- Level 1 126
- Level 2 127
- Level 3 130
- Three Little Birds 133
- Angry Bird 134

Week 6 136
- Level 1 136
- Level 2 137
- Level 3 139
- Three Little Birds 141
- Angry Bird 143

Week 7 143
- Level 1 143
- Level 2 145
- Level 3 147
- Three Little Birds 150
- Angry Bird 151

Week 8 151
- Level 1 151
- Level 2 153
- Level 3 155

Three Little Birds 159
Angry Bird 160
Rock and Roll – More Practice Problems 161

About the author

Udar Nivol is an IT Analyst specialized in delivering data warehousing and business intelligence applications serving a variety of financial services including leasing, insurance, banking, finance intelligence, anti-money laundering.

He was a Math Olympian during his school years in Eastern Europe. When his son turned 7 and started the 2nd grade, Udar realized that Math was not taught in schools as it used to be when he was at his son's age. He thought it was his responsibility as a parent to ensure his kids were exposed to at least the same level of education as he was. This book is the result of the weekly meetings he had with his son and his son's colleagues. And as the name of the book suggests, it is an experiment. We'll see how far along can a group of smart kids can go when they are exposed to more difficult math word problems and compete in Math contests. This is the first book of the Math Experiment series. Please join them and read about their achievements, challenges, and milestones. Week by week. Year by year.

Udar currently lives along with his wife and 2 kids in Michigan, enjoying the Great Lakes' serene beaches in the summer, and the crisp, starry and clear nights of Upper Peninsula in the winter.

For Gene, Sydney, Trenton, Vlad and their unbridled minds.

Why this book?

"There is something wrong happening with our kids"

It was the summer before my son entered the second grade when I first thought of writing this book. The Olympic Games were going on at that time and all the sport fans were glued to their TV sets or checking the results online. We were watching the games amazed by the determination of those athletes, and I was telling my son how hard they worked to get there, how many hours they spent in trainings and how many things they gave up. He watched them in awe and was already putting together a short list of personal heroes: Michael Phelps, Usain Bolt, Rafael Nadal, Hope Solo, Gabby Douglas, Missy Franklin...And while my son was plowing the Internet in search for his new heroes' birth dates and places, training schedules, hobbies and schools they attended, I was thinking of the coming fall. Second grade. I felt at loss of how I was going to handle that. I have to admit that I was afraid, because I looked around me and I realized that the kids nowadays don't learn as we used to do when we were like them. I had desperately tried to find reasons for that. I read dozens of books, talked to child psychologists, parents, teachers, leaders of homeschool organization, scientists, but I can't say I have a definite answer. What I can say for sure is that a lot of things have changed since I was at my son's age and we are all witnesses to them– culture, technology, entertainment, attention span, food, curriculum, responsibilities, the pace of day to day life.

There is one statement that I hear quite often and has already become a cliché: "there is something wrong happening with our kids' Math and Science education nowadays". I hear it in talk shows, presidential campaigns, at NPR, you name it. And the more we hear about it, the more we refer to it as a fact. There's really not much we can do about it, it's just a fact.

"I think we have become complacent. We've sort of lost our way. We are lagging the rest of the world, and we are lagging it in pretty substantial ways. "
- Arne Duncan, Secretary of Education

Some people started to look at other countries, particularly in Asia, to understand what it is that they do better than the US.

"The United States is failing to develop the math skills of both girls and boys, especially among those who could excel at the highest levels, a new study asserts, and girls who do succeed in the field are almost all immigrants or the daughters of immigrants from countries where mathematics is more highly valued."
- New York Times

The administrations came up with radical education strategies:

"The National Assessment of Educational Progress found fourth-graders had made no learning gains since the last time the NAEP math test was given, in 2007. Previously, fourth-graders had made scoring gains on every NAEP math test given since 1990. In a statement, Secretary of Education Arne Duncan called the NAEP results "unacceptable," and said they underscore the

need for "reforms that will accelerate student achievement." While not focused specifically on math, the Obama administration's education strategy calls for adopting tougher measures, such as opening more charter schools and linking teacher pay to performance."
- Wall Street Journal

There is nothing wrong with our teachers

I was very well aware of all this, but I had not really paid very much attention to it until my son started the school. The school was great but I wanted to be proactive and try to find potential flaws. Of course, I started with the teachers - the easiest target, they deal directly with our kids. Well, I was wrong. The majority of teachers that I have met made a positive impression on me. I have all the admiration in the world for what they do. I sense a feeling of humbleness when I sit next to them in the parent-teacher conferences. They have a huge responsibility that goes beyond following the curriculum and making sure the students pass the tests. They have to inspire, to make the students ask for more, to provide role models and make them understand that there's something out there that can't be found on Facebook, there is no app for it and no computer game to emulate it. It is the knowledge. It can be grasped only with passion, patience and thirst for learning and it is the only source for progress. And it is not only the teachers who have this responsibility. The parents play a huge role too. If we can provide this to our kids, half of the problem is solved. And indeed, I started to perceive this new tendency lately. We slowed down blaming each other and talking about wrong curriculum, wrong school systems, unmotivated teachers, lazy students, the influence of TV programs and video games, and started to talk more about what we can change from within:

"Teachers must inspire; principals must lead; parents must instill a thirst for learning, and students, you've gotta do the work. And together, I promise you, we can out-educate and out-compete any nation on Earth. Help me recruit 100,000 math and science teachers within ten years, and improve early childhood education."
- Barack Obama, Democratic National Convention , 2012

It is our mentality that we have to fight with

There is a whole paradigm that needs to be shifted here, in the US and not only. We often hear people say "math was never my strong suit" or "I was never good at math" or, even worse, "school sucks". There were times when one would have felt ashamed to say that. But now it became trendy. There are countries where the young math wizards are respected and considered role models. In the US and other western countries, they are just a bunch of boring nerds. What caused this shift? Pop culture? Hollywood? Media? I don't know, I let the sociologists answer.

"There's just a stigma in this country about math being really hard and feared, and people who do it being strange. It's particularly hard for girls, especially at the ages when people start doing competitions. If you look at schools, there is often a social group of nerdy boys. There's that image of what it is to be a nerdy boy in mathematics. It's still in some way socially unacceptable for boys, but at least it's a position and it's clearly defined."
- Melanie Wood, the first girl who ever made it to the US Math Olympic Team, in 1998, cited by New York Times

Let's put the Village back together

I remember my small town in Easter Europe from beyond the Iron Curtain, quivering with excitement when the Math contests were approaching. The Math Olympics were on everyone's lips, and the excitement grew bigger and bigger as the students went through eliminatory contests – the school contest, then town, county, country and only the best from the best were qualified to go to the International Olympiad. It was everyone's dream, the supreme achievement, the recognition of a very hard work and talent. The public school was in the middle of all this action. Everything was driven by the school and the teachers who were willing to spend countless unpaid hours to train the students for these contests. Their prestige and fame were at stake, as well as their professional and human fulfillment.

30 years later and 12,000 miles away from my low-paced childhood town, which, by the way, is now also touched by this global complacency, I find myself in a very difficult position. I'm trying to pass on to my kids everything that I now perceive was valuable in my upbringing. This is something that all the parents do. We feel obliged to do so. But it takes a village to raise a kid, doesn't it? Well, I miss the village. I can only find bits and pieces of it and it's our duty, as responsible parents, to put everything back together again. It's getting harder nowadays to find real role models for the kids to look up to, fruitful passions that they can hold on to, fierce but good and respectful competition between students, strong drive to achieve great things, recognition of the true values. I grew up in a communist country and obviously not all the values that were promoted at that time were true. My parents had to unclutter my brain, as subtly as they could, of all the propaganda and the lies told us by the regime's leaders, and always advised me to embrace science. In science, one can never lie. A hypothesis is either true or false. There is no middle way. One can solve a problem in many ways but the answer is always the same. And that's what I did; I followed my parents' advice. Math became my favorite subject; I treated it like a game and a continuous discovery. I was exhilarated every time I could solve a difficult problem, and I also cried with despair when I couldn't. But I never gave up. I had colleagues who were gifted, a lot smarter than me, but that never discouraged me. I took it as a challenge and opportunity to learn something from them and to set my goals higher and higher. And when I did better than them in contests, I had that sweet and incomparable feeling of achievement. Even today I believe that competition is the main engine of progress. Later on, in college, I discovered computers, algorithms and their perfect marriage with math. I got my first job while I was still in college. I am now in my 30s and I have already lived and worked on 3 continents, met great people and amazing professionals, made great friends across the world, and used my knowledge in very challenging and interesting projects. Did the advice given by my parents pay off? It certainly did. Can I do the same with my kid? I certainly can. But will the seed sown by me find a fertile soil? Well, I'll have to take care of that too. It's harder to find fertile soil nowadays than one generation ago. We, the parents, have to fertilize it with a lot of love, patience and passion.

Back to my lost village, yes, I'm still on the look for it, and while I do that, I feel the strong urge to take the reins in my hands and try to do as much as I can. I met a lot of parents who, for one reason or another, were homeschooling their kids. I have all the respect and admiration for them. 2 mil kids were homeschooled in 2012 (http://homeschooling.gomilpitas.com/weblinks/numbers.htm#.UbdHtOfVDj4) and the growth rate averages around 5% every year. I, for one, couldn't do that. But at east I'll make sure I'll share with my kids all the math that my teachers thought me when I was at their age. I'll try to instill the love for math and science just like my teachers did. This book talks about my attempt and the long journey that awaits me.

Coming back to the Olympic Games, my son was very eager to share with me information he found on Internet about his new heroes. Gabby Douglas - the first American gymnast to win gold in both the individual all-around and team competitions at the same Olympics; Michael Phelps – the most decorated Olympian of all time, 22 medals," can you believe, dad?"; Usain Bolt – the fastest person ever, the first man to win 6 Olympic gold medals in sprinting, and the list went on and on.

I thought this was the perfect time to introduce my son to other heroes, Olympians too, but how haven't been much on the spotlight. They don't make appearances in TV shows, nor do they make it to the magazines covers. They live their quiet lives, going from one scholarship to another, writing their research papers, or even working in the R&D departments of Fortune 500 companies.

The Math Olympians

How many people know who **Melanie Wood** is? Just like the other renowned Olympians, she worked very hard and won medals for US. She was the first female American to make the US International Math Olympiad Team, receiving silver medals in the 1998 and 1999 International Mathematical Olympiad.

How about **Terence Tao**, from Australia, the youngest medalist in the history of the Math Olympiad? He won bronze when he was 10, silver at 11, and gold at 12. He learned how to count from Elmo TV shows.

Ciprian Manolescu, from Romania, was the only person to achieve 3 perfect scores at International Math Olympiad.

The Serbian **Teodor van Burk** is for Math what is Michael Phelps for swimming. Teodor is the most successful participant if the International Math Olympiad, with 4 gold, 1 silver and 1 bronze medals.

These are only few examples but there are so many math prodigies out there who can become the perfect role models for our kids. We only have to let our kids know about them and encourage them to try. Let's take them to competitions. Or at least let's make them aware about them. How many kids know that there is an International Math Olympiad where all the top notch math wizards (not nerds) from around the world meet every year? How many know about Putnam Competition where the top scores holders get thousands of dollars in prizes and get their tuition waved at top universities in the country? How many know about math camps organized by former math Olympians and Putnam fellows? I again have to refer to one of the Wood's interviews:

"If it hadn't been for a teacher asking me, 'Hey, do you want to come to this math competition?' I would have never stumbled into it naturally because my friends weren't in a math club after school or anything."

This is when she started to win math competitions. It happened because she was exposed to them by her teacher.

So this is what this book is all about:

- Provide role models - stories about math prodigies from old and our times

- Facts about all the math competitions across the US and not only

- Attempt to create a framework for success, with math problems, strategies and solutions. It is just an attempt and the name of book justifies that. The goal of this experiment is to inspire the love for math and help kids win medals, prizes and be proud of their achievements. We'll see how far along we can get and we invite you, the reader, to be the witness and the judge.

- If you decide to take some action and run a math club for 2nd graders, this book will give you everything you need – curriculum, problems, drills, approach, tests, information about math competitions, tips and things I did wrong

The experiment and organization of the book

The experiment consists in forming a small group of second graders who otherwise would not have exposure to any math competitions, and having them accustomed to several types of math word problems and strategies to solve them. We will then participate in contests and compete against other students across the country. And since this is an experiment, we'll have to treat it as such, so we will document all the steps, get feedback, measure the progress, and tweak the inputs to obtain the desired outputs. In the end, we'll summarize all the results and decide whether the experiment was successful or not, based on 3 criteria:

- Number of medals and certificates

- The attained math culture (the students should be able to have a conversation about several renowned math personalities and famous stories)

- Knowledge about math competitions (the students should have preferences formed for one competition or another and be able to reason their preferences)

The organization of the book

The book is divided in weekly sections. The math club meets every week for an hour and we discuss a particular topic. Every section will have the following 5 parts:

- **Letter to the Parents** – A quick recap of the kids studied during that week's session.
- **The story** – The students will be introduced to a Math personality or a famous Math concept, listen to a story, or watch a Math related movie.
- **Curriculum** – The coach will present the concept and the problems, lead the discussion about the solutions and strategies. The problems will be presented in gradual fashion, according to their level of difficulty (more on that later).
- **Three Little Birds** – A 3 problem test to review the concepts learned in the previous sessions. The test will be graded and the students will accumulate points for all the problems correctly solved. The first student who accumulates a predefined number of points, will get a prize. No, the name has nothing to do with Bob Marley.
- **The Angry Bird** - This is a challenge problem that requires more intense mental effort and attention to detail. The student who solves this problem gets a prize on the spot. No, the name has nothing to do with the Angry Birds game.

The weekly meets are one hour long and obviously there wouldn't be enough time to cover all the information above. The coach can choose and pick. We had in total 19 weekly sessions, but I comprised everything in only 8 chapters in this book. So you can't really cover in one hour everything I included in one chapter. We'll talk more about this in Week 0 – Getting started with the Math Club.

There will be a chapter on Math competitions and another one on reviewing all the accomplishments and deciding whether the experiment was successful or not. The chapter "Rock and Roll" has more problems from different categories for the kids to solve and become familiar with the Math concepts presented in the other chapters. The chapter "Results and Solutions" will have detailed solutions for all the problems presented throughout the book.

The Problems

The problems are structured in several categories based on their type and solving strategy. There are 4 levels of difficulty for every curriculum entry. Level 1 and 2 problems are designed to reinforce the concepts learned at school. Level 3 problems are more difficult and different from what the students learned at school. Level 4 problems are only included in the Angry Problem section and the Rock and Roll chapter.

All the problems on this book will have an identifier to suggest the category and the level. For instance ML3-023 refers the problem number 23 in the "More or Less" category, Lever 3. The problems in Rock and Roll chapter are presented as RR-nnn. The students will have to find the category and apply the appropriate strategy.

Here's an example of how the problems will be gradually introduced to the students in the "More or Less" category:

Level 1: ML1-001. Olivia has 22 stickers, and she has 8 fewer than her brother Sam. How many stickers does Sam have?

Level 2: ML2-001. The U8 team in the Rochester Soccer Club has 3 first graders and 9 second graders. How many more second graders are there in the team?

Level 3: ML3-001. There are 15 children in the North Hill Math Club. There are 3 more girls than boys in the club. How many girls are in the club?

Level 4: PR-001. John, Olivia and Ken are the top 3 students in a math tournament. They will all get medals: gold for 1st place, silver for 2nd place, bronze for 3rd place. John and Ken together accumulated 10 points. Ken had 4 more points than John, and Olivia had 2 less points than Ken. What medal is Olivia going to get and with what score?

A parent of one of the children who are part of this experiment sent me a very interesting article (http://www.artofproblemsolving.com/Resources/articles.php?page=pc_competitions) that talks about the pros and cons of math competitions. I won't talk about the advantages (you can read about them in the article), but I'll just briefly refer the 3 pitfalls mentioned there:

1. **Not all the contests are designed well**. The author refers to those contests that promote speed and memorization. "Do 30 additions in less than a minute" type of thing. This is something that I'll never encourage. In fact I withdrew my son from a math club (I won't say the name but it is one of the popular ones, with centers in every city) that uses these techniques. Memorization is good up to a point, then you have to make room for creativity.
2. **Extending kids beyond their ability**. This can really be a serious problem, because the kids can get discouraged and then they will try to distant themselves from everything related to Math. This is the reason I tend to tackle every category in a gradual manner,

starting with Level 1, 2, 3. The students will pass to level 4 only if they are fully comfortable with the problems in first 3 levels.

3. **Participants in math contests are just as much at risk of burnout as musicians or athletes**. If the students show any signs of fatigue, we'll back out immediately. I'll be in permanent touch with the parents. We may even skip some competitions if the parents decide so.

Week 0 – Getting started with the Math Club

I sent an email to the principal of the school that my son was attending, and I explained my intentions. Here's the email that I sent, followed by the principal's reply:

Dear Mr. Principal,

I wasn't sure whom I should address this email to, so I'm sending it to you, hoping that you will forward it to the right person. I have a proposal to make and I hope you'll find it appealing, as it refers to an after school activity that doesn't require any additional cost and may make our school visible not only in Michigan, but across the country. I would like to put together a Math Club with 2nd graders where we'll discuss different strategies to solve word problems. The team will compete in several national math contests throughout the year (please see the list below). We'll promote logical and strategic thinking, fair competition and attention to details. The students will learn how to compete against each other, as they will get a score every week, based on a short test and, in the same time, they will learn how to act as a team when they compete against other teams across the nation.

The club will follow the 2nd grade math curriculum, we'll start with the basic concepts that are taught in the class, but then we'll raise the level a couple of notches to cover the complexity of the problems given at contests.

In short, this is what the students will learn:

- Strategies to solve word problems
- Types of word problems - the students will be able to recognize these types and apply the appropriate strategies
- I'll also try to spice the classes with stories about great mathematicians and math Olympians to keep their interest kindled.

These are some of the strategies that we'll discuss about:

- Logical reasoning
- Model with diagrams
- Work backwards
- Solve a simpler problem
- Guess and check

There are quite a few national math contests throughout the year, but we'll only focus on the 3 major ones:

- Continental Math League (http://www.continentalmathematicsleague.com/)
- Math Kangaroo (http://www.mathkangaroo.org/2010page/kangur/main.htm)
- Noetic Learning Math Contest (http://www.noetic-learning.com/mathcontest/)

The parents will get weekly emails with updates about the class and their kids' progress.

The students will have the opportunity to earn individual and team medals and certificates. No traveling will be required, the tests will be proctored by me or any other teacher, and then the results will be sent over to the each contest's committee and published on their websites. And, as I said in the beginning, there won't be any costs involved. I'll support all the expenses for the team.

The reason I want to do this with 2nd graders is easy to understand (my son is one of them), but we can look at this endeavor like at a pilot project, and once we have in place a successful framework, maybe we can replicate it to other grades.

Thanks for your time and I look forward to meeting you in person.

Principal's Reply:

Thank you for expressing interest in offering this opportunity to our students. However they are already involved in the Math Pentathlon throughout most of the school year. Mrs. B. (parent) leads this program. To offer another math program may cause competition between the two programs. If you are interested in assisting with Math Pentathlon please let me know and I will send you Mrs. B's contact information.

Thank you,

He was right and I perfectly understood his argument. It could have definitely generated a conflict. Math Pentathlon was a great program, but it was essentially a set of games, and I wanted something more for my son. Now, in the hindsight, I don't think that sending an email to the principal was a good idea. What if he embraced the idea and 20-30 kids signed up for the new club? I'm not sure I could have handled that because I didn't have a tested framework in place. Now I can say for sure that I can handle it, this book provides everything one would need to run a Math club for 2nd graders. So I sent emails to few of the parents that I knew from other school activities. I received a positive answer from 3 of them and we were all set to start our adventure. I had 4 kids in my little Math Club (my son was the 4th one).

Few days after that, the principal had a second thought and was kind enough to send me another email asking for more details. He wanted to approach the parent teacher association with my proposal. But this time I politely backed out because I didn't really know what to expect from an enrolment perspective. And besides that, I had everything I needed for my little experiment.

I booked a study room at the local public library, prepared handouts and the agenda for the first session. My goal for the first session was to spark the interest, because I really wanted them to do all this with pleasure and curiosity. I bought a white board because another goal of mine was to teach them from this early age, how to present a solution. This is a skill that gradually becomes extinct nowadays, when most of the problems are presented in multiple choice tests. I also created a website to track the progress and keep everything within easy reach. This is how www.mathexperiment.com came into being.

The kids have all different interests and personalities. One is in an absolute love for numbers; if he could play with them all day long, he would be the happiest kid in town. I'll refer to him in this book as the **Number Cruncher**. The second one seems to be more inclined towards technology; when I explained in our first session how the Saturn V rocket worked, he was mesmerized. He asked a lot of pertinent questions and he wanted to make sure he understood everything. I'll call him the **Engineer**. The third kid likes to present solutions on the white board. I'll call him the **Presenter**. The only girl in the group is joyful and exuberant. I'll call her **Joy**. Now let's rock!

Week 1

Week 1 Letter to the Parents

The first session went quite well I would say. We didn't do all that I had in plan to do, but we did enough. The kids were very excited to spend time together in an environment other than the school.

I started talking a little bit about the stuff they did at school - math boxes and number facts ("the triangles", as the kids call them).

Then we talked about the Apollo 13 space mission and how the astronauts used their math skills and solving strategies to overcome all problems and get back to Earth safe. We watched together the Apollo 13 movie trailer.

There is one thing that I have to get better at. Their attention span is still limited at this age, especially when they are together and try to entertain each other, and if I didn't keep them engaged every bit of time, they start drifting away. I think I learned a great deal from this first session as to how to deal with these young and unbridled minds. It's not a walk in the park, let me tell you that! One more reason to take my hat off to all the teachers who do this on a daily basis.

Then we went through the "More or Less" problems. The Level 1 and Level 2 problems were relatively easy to solve after the kids understood the technique. This kind of problems will never be given at contests, but they laid the foundation for the following level. Level 3 problems are a little bit more difficult but, again, once the kids understood the 2 strategies I gave them, they could solve them without any struggle. The students learned that there might be different ways to solve a problem, but the solution will always be the same. We debated a little bit on what strategy would be faster and more straightforward.

I gave the kids worksheets with Level 1, 2, 3 strategies and practice problems.

Week 1 Story – Apollo 13

Apollo program was a set of missions for traveling in the outer space, beyond the low Earth orbit (that's around 1,200 miles above the ground). The program was carried out by NASA (National Aeronautics and Space Administration) and it was a huge endeavor, involving a lot of scientists - physicists, mathematicians, chemists, engineers and so on. The program was initiated by President Eisenhower (1953 - 1961) and continued by President Kennedy (1961 -1963), President Johnson (1963 - 1969), and President Nixon (1969 -1974). President Kennedy proposed the national goal of "landing a man on the Moon and returning him safely to the Earth" by the end of the 1969.

The goal was accomplished with the Apollo 11 mission (the 5th manned mission), when the astronauts Neil Armstrong and Buzz Aldrin walked on the moon for the first time in the humankind history, on July 20, 1969. There were 12 manned Apollo missions in all and 6 of them landed astronauts on the moon.

The 7th manned Apollo mission didn't go as planned. The craft was launched on April 11, 1970 and it had the scope of flying to the moon and do more exploring. It was the 3rd mission intended to land on the Moon. The crew was composed of James A. Lovell (commander), John L. Swigert (Command Module pilot) and Fred W. Haise (Lunar Module pilot).

The 3 members of the Apollo 13 Mission. Credit NASA (Source: http://www.apolloarchive.com/apollo_gallery.html)

After 3 days and 200,000 miles, one of the 2 blocks of oxygen exploded due to some thermostatic switches that were not upgraded. Those switches were supposed to initiate the cooling when the temperature reached 80 degrees F, but because they didn't work, the temperature reached 1000 F degrading the insulation during a test on the ground and causing the explosion during the mission.

A loud bang let the astronauts thought that they were hit by a meteorite. The astronauts had to quickly assess the problem. The oxygen for the no 1 tank leaked into space. With the oxygen gone, there would be no more air to breath and there would be no more fuel to generate electricity. The command module was now running on battery power only. And the battery lifetime was very limited and vital for landing back to Earth.

The astronauts had to use the problem solving strategies they learned in school and during the training to save their lives.

1. What is the initial set of facts?
2. What is it that we need to solve?
3. Which parts of the problem appear to be the most critical to finding a solution?
4. Is there some information that can be ignored?
5. Present the solution and verify the results.

This solving strategy can be used for any math problem, although we would only need steps 1, 2, and 5 most of the times.

They had to shut down the command volume and moved to the lunar module.

Passing through the tunnel from Command Module to Lunar Module. Credit NASA.

The commander quickly made the calculations required to activate the lunar module ahead of time and to establish the right course to use the Moon's gravity to return to Earth. These calculations were never written before and never tested. They couldn't afford to make mistakes. It was their lives that he made the calculations for. The manual where he wrote down the calculations was sold in an auction in 2011 for $388,375. It represented an example of high determination, strategic thinking and extraordinary math skills. Those calculations were crucial to put the ship on the course that would return it to Earth.

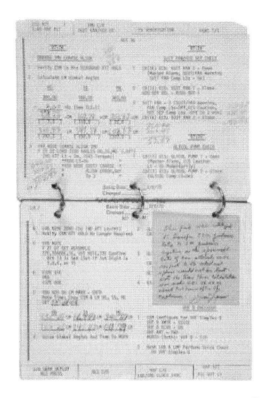

The manual where Commander Lovell made the calculations. Credit NASA.

The electrical power was the most important aspect they needed in order to survive. They had to conserve as much energy as possible. So they stopped the live broadcast, turned down the heaters, and limited the radio communication with Earth.

Back on Earth, the people in the control center were working around the clock. They determined how much time they had to keep the astronauts on board alive. They calculated backwards form the time all the resources of life were depleted and made their decision based on that.

They used charts, drawing and calculations.

The control center confirmed all the numbers and the astronauts began their journey back home. Few other things went wrong, but the courage and training of the astronauts combined with the genius and dedicated team work down on Earth finally saved the day, making Apollo 13 the most successful failure in the history of the space program.

Apollo 13 Movie Trailer:

http://www.youtube.com/watch?v=nEloNsYn1fU

Week 1 Curriculum – More or Less

To recognize this kind of problems, look for the keywords "more", "less", "fewer", "longer", "shorter", "taller", "higher", "lower", "younger", "older" etc.

Level 1

ML1-001 Olivia has 22 stickers, and she has 8 **fewer** than her brother Sam. How many stickers does Sam have?

We'll follow the steps below to solve any kind of problem. At this age, the students will have to draw a lot, because this is the best way they can understand and come up with a solution. Note the highlighted keywords. They always give us clues about the type of the problem.

Identify the subjects

Olivia (O) and Sam (S)

Sketch the facts. What do we know about the subjects?

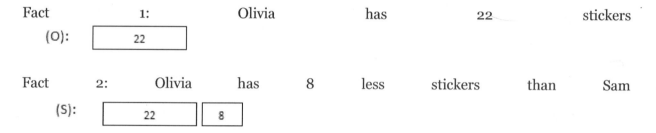

Write the solution

So Sam has 22 + 8 = 30 stickers.

ML1-002 Olivia has 22 stickers, and she has 8 **more** than her brother Sam. How many stickers does Sam have?

Identify the subjects

Olivia (O) and Sam (S)

Sketch the facts. What do we know about the subjects?

Fact 1: Olivia has 22 stickers
Fact 2: Olivia has 8 stickers more than her brother Sam.

So we'll have to take away 8 stickers from Olivia's 22 to find out how many stickers Sam has.

Write the solution

(S): 22 − 8 = 14 stickers

Sam has 14 stickers.

Now the student should try to solve the following problems without help:

ML1-003 Jack bought a pirates puzzle that had 20 pieces **less than** the cars puzzle which he already had. The pirates puzzle had 50 pieces. How many pieces did the cars puzzle have?

Identify the subjects
Sketch the facts. What do we know about the subjects?
Write the solution

ML1-004 Justin and his sister, Helen went shopping. Justin bought 60 markers. If he bought 20 **fewer** markers than his sister, how many did Helen buy?

ML1-005 Gene bought a donut that was 15 cents less expensive than a muffin. The price of the donut was 25 cents. How much did the muffin cost?

ML1-006 For the art class, the teacher brought some red and blue ribbons. There are 5 fewer blue ribbons than red ribbons. If there are 12 blue ribbons, how many red ribbons are there?

ML1-007 At the grocery store, an apple costs 50 cents. The price of the apple is 25 cents higher than the price of the banana. How much does the banana costs?

ML1-008. Trenton's desk is 90 centimeters tall. The desk is 30 centimeters taller than his chair. How tall is his chair?

ML1-009. Vlad picked 15 apples and some peaches from the orchard. He picked 7 more peaches than apples. How many peaches did he harvest?

ML1-010. Mother is 26 years younger than Grandpa and she is now 30 years old. How old is Grandpa?

Level 2

ML2-011. John got 12 balloons from the fair. His sister, Olivia, got 8 balloons. **How many fewer** did Olivia get?

Identify the subjects

John (J) and Olivia (O)

Sketch the facts. What do we know about the subjects?

Fact 1: John has 12 balloons

Fact 2: Olivia has 8 balloons

(J) [12]
(O) [8]

How many balloons does Olivia need in order to have the same number of balloons as her brother?

(J) [12]
(O) [8][?]

8 + ? = 12

Write the solution

The answer is 12-8=4 balloons.

ML2-012. Gene scored 8 goals during the soccer game last Saturday. Vlad scored 3 goals. How many fewer goals did Vlad score?

Identify the subjects
Sketch the facts. What do we know about the subjects?
Write the solution

ML2-013. Dwayne is 55 inches tall. His younger brother, Dustin, is 40 inches tall. How much shorter is Dustin?

ML2-014. An helicopter can fly up to 1,000 feet above the ground. A commercial airplane can go to 6,000 feet above the ground. How much higher can the airplane fly?

ML2-015. Adam is 8 years old. His grandpa is 78. How much older is his grandpa?

ML2-016. In the professional soccer leagues, the goals are 8 yards wide. In the youth leagues, they can be 3 yards wide. How much wider are the goals used in the professional soccer leagues?

ML2-017. A sack of beans weighs 20 pounds. A bag of lentils weighs 28 pounds. How much heavier are the lentils?

ML2-018. Trenton and Sydney are getting ready for the Math Pentathlon tournament. They play a Hex-A-Gone game together. Trenton has placed 7 pieces on the board and 2 of them were hexagons. Sydney placed 10 pieces and 4 of them were diamonds. How many more pieces did Sydney place on the board?

Hint: Think of the strategies used by Apollo 13 astronauts. Is there some information that can be ignored? They didn't have to bother about oxygen, they had plenty of it. It was only the electrical power that they lacked. Is there anything in this problem that you can ignore?

ML2-019. Maia and John counted the money in their piggy banks. Maia has $5.37 and John has $10.15. How much more money does John have?

ML2-020. Daria solved 297 math problems over the summer. Vlad solved 119. How many less problems did Vlad solve than Daria?

Level 3

The students should have by now the skills required to tackle the problems in Level 3. These problems don't provide any information about the individual subjects like it happened in the previous levels. They only provide details about all the subjects clubbed together and how they differ from one another. This kind of problems will be solved in the higher grades using systems of equations, but this is not to say that they can't be solved using 2nd grade skills. There are actually 2 strategies that the students can chose from. Both are intuitive and easy to apply.

ML3-021. There are 15 children in the North Hill Math Club. There are 3 **more** girls than boys in the club. How many girls are there in the club?

Strategy 1 (Sketch the facts)

Identify the subjects

Boys (B) and Girls (G)

Sketch the facts. What do we know about the subjects?

Fact 1: There are 3 more girls than boys.

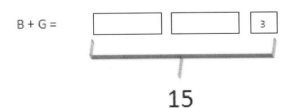

Fact2: We know that there are 15 kids altogether. So let's put them all together now:

B + G = [ ] [ ] [3]
         └──────15──────┘

Can we now find out the value of the 2 rectangles put together?

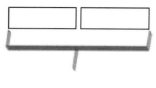

$15 - 3 = 12$

So now we can get the value of just one rectangle. What's the half of

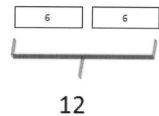

12?

Write the solution

Let's now go back to the Fact 1 and write the result:

B: [6]   = 6 boys

G: [6][3]   = 9 girls

Always check the results:
Fact 1: Are the girls 3 more than the boys? Yes (9 = 6 + 3)
Fact 2: Are they 15 altogether? Yes (6 + 9 = 15)

Strategy 2 (Trial and Error)

So we know that total number of boys and girls together is 15, and the girls are 3 more than the boys. Let's pick just a number of boys and check the facts. Obviously, the number has to be less than 15 so we leave some room for girls too. See the comments in the table below.

	Boys	Girls (3 more)	Total	Comment
Trial 1	9	12	21	Too much, try again with fewer boys
Trial 2	8	11	19	Too much, try again with fewer boys
Trial 3	5	8	13	Less than 15, try again with more boys
Trial 4	6	9	15	Perfect!

ML3-022 Mr. Vlassopoulos uses 20 balls in his sports class. There are 8 more soccer balls than tennis balls. How many soccer balls is he using?

Strategy 1

Identify the subjects

Sketch the facts. What do we know about the subjects?

Write the solution

Strategy 2

	Boys	Girls	Total	Comment
Trial 1				
Trial 2				
Trial 3				
Trial 4				
Trial 5				

ML3-023 Hana and Diane arranged their jumping cords head to head and measured them. The two cords together measured 110 inches. Hana's cord is 30 inches shorter than Diane's. How long is Diane's cord?

ML3-024. Gene and Sydney put their money together to buy a board game. They had 17 dollars together. Gene had 3 dollars more than Sydney. How much money did Sydney have?

ML3-025. The ages of Jack's mom and dad add up to 64 years. His dad is 4 years older than his mom. How old is his mom?

ML3-026. There are 123 white and black marbles in a jar. The number of white marbles is 47 greater than the number of black marbles. How many white marbles are in the jar?

ML3-027. Uncle John has apple trees and cherry trees in his orchard, 46 in all. There are 12 more apple trees than cherry trees. How many cherry trees does Uncle John have?

ML3-028. The students in Mrs. Mustola class have to arrange the tables and the chairs in the school's festivity hall. They counted 76 tables and chairs together. There are 38 more chairs than tables. How many tables are there in the festivity hall?

ML3-029. Daria went to the farmers market and bought apples and peaches. She counted them all and got 87 fruits. She bought 29 more apples than peaches. How many apples did she buy?

ML3-030. Vlad's grandpa raises sheep and cows in his farm. There are 45 animals altogether and there are 19 more sheep than cows. How many sheep does the grandpa have?

Week 1 Three Little Birds

LB-031 Vlad has 6 more pencils than Gene. Sydney has as many pencils as Vlad and Gene have together. If Vlad has 13 pencils, how many pencils does Sydney have?

LB-032 Vlad and Daria worked on their homework together yesterday. Vlad had to complete 27 math problems and Daria 36 problems. They took a break right after Vlad finished 10 problems and Daria finished 12 problems. How many less problems did Vlad completed after the break than Daria did after the break?

LB-033 Vlad has 23 balloons and Sydney has 32. If Sydney will give Vlad 8 balloons, she will have ___ less balloons than Vlad.

Week 1 Angry Bird

AB-034 Vivian, Alex and Sophie have 140 balloons altogether. Vivian and Alex have the same number of balloons. Alex and Sophie have together 82 balloons. How many balloons does Alex have?

Week 2

Week 2 Letter to the Parents

We had a good, solid hour of math this time. No distractions and no drifting away. I think I'm getting better at this. The secret is to keep them engaged all the time, cutting short any tendency of mind-wandering. When I feel the student is about to start drifting away, I quickly ask him a question to make the wheels spin again. The challenge comes up when I have to explain a problem a second time to a student who didn't understand it. Then I have to keep the others busy somehow.

We started as usually with what they did at school this week. I asked them what a function machine was and they jumped right away to explain me how it worked! The Presenter couldn't wait to sketch it on the white board, so I let him do it.

The Number Cruncher surprised me again. He brought a sheet half full of Fibonacci numbers! He wanted to show me how they work. Next time I am going to tell them more about Fibonacci.

Then we delved into the Dates and Times module. We talked about birth dates, ages, how we determine who is older and who is younger. I asked them to write their ages on a piece of paper and tell me what the sum of their ages is going to be in 2015. I was hoping someone would say "Well, that depends on what month in 2015...". No one did, and I didn't have time to challenge them. I'll do it next time. The Engineer was very quick on doing all the calculations in his head.

I showed the kids how they can always remember how many days a month has. They enjoyed the knuckles method more than the mnemonic.

We briefly talked about the different date formats used in the word. The students should always work with dates in M-D-Y format (the American format). However The US are among the very few countries that use it. The majority of the countries use D-M-Y format (known as the British format). I showed the kids a map with dates formats used across the world (http://en.wikipedia.org/wiki/Date_format_by_country).

There are 3 more weeks until the first contest – Noetic Math Fall Contest. So at this point we'll have to stop our schedule and work on the problems given in the past years, so the students will get familiarized with them. We'll try to cover as much as we can.

I am going to book a big conference room at the public library on Saturday, November 3rd, between 1 PM and 3 PM. Students will have 45 minutes to work on the problems.

That's it for now; I'll send another update next week.

Week 2 Story – The Number of Days in Each Month

The number of days in each month has remained unchanged for 2000 years (since 45 B.C. in fact, when Julius Caesar introduced the Julian Calendar). Here's a well-known mnemonic rhyme which has been in existence for over 400 years, to indicate the exact number of days in each different month:

30 days hath September,
  April, June and November,
All the rest have 31,
  Excepting February alone
(And that has 28 days clear,
  With 29 in each leap year).

http://www.youtube.com/watch?v=drH3_Flt85g

The number of days in each month can also be found by counting across the knuckles and valleys on the back of each clenched fist (from left to right):

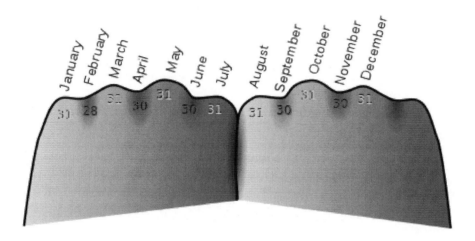

Each "knuckle" month has 31 days, while each "valley" month has only 30 days (excepting of course February).

Each month-name originated from the Roman calendar and mostly from the pre-Julian calendar when the year started with March and ended with February. September was Septilis (Latin for 'seventh month') and is still the seventh month counting from March. Similarly October, November and December mean 'eighth, ninth, and tenth month'. The fifth month was Quinctilis until it was renamed Julius (hence July) in honor of Julius Caesar, whereupon his successor, the emperor Augustus, renamed Sextilis after himself too (hence August). Augustus also added a day to August (making 31) so as match that for Julius! Here's how the Senate justified this decision:

"Whereas the Emperor Augustus Caesar, in the month of Sextillis . . . thrice entered the city in triumph . . . and in the same month Egypt was brought under the authority of the Roman people, and in the same month an end was put to the civil wars; and whereas for these reasons the said month is, and has been, most fortunate to this empire, it is hereby decreed by the senate that the said month shall be called Augustus."

The remaining months are either named after Roman gods (Janus, Mars, Maia, Juno) or have a religious significance (Februarius meaning 'purification month' before the new year cycle, and Aprilis being connected to well-being and prosperity). February had originally 29 or 30 days, but after Augustus decided to add 1 day to the his month, he took it from February, since it was the last month of the Roman calendar before 45 BC anyway. These Romans…

Week 2 Curriculum – Dates and Times

Level 1

The problems in the first level are meant to re-enforce the general concepts learned in the math class: how many minutes in an hour, how many days in a week, how many months or weeks in a year and so on.

Also, the students have to be very confident when they talk about fast-slow and old-young concepts. A lot of the kids get confused here when they are exposed first time to these problems because somehow they are wired to know that the more they have, the better. Whereas here, the shorter the time, the faster it goes. The same goes with old-young. The youngest guys have the greatest year of birth.

Let's start with few examples:

DT01-035. Which of the following statements are true?
A. One day is shorter than 20 hours.
B. 3 weeks make a period of time shorter than 2 months
C. 18 days make a period of time longer than 3 weeks

With such type of problems, a comparison is required between 2 or more different units of time. The rule of thumb is to **convert the greater time unit into the smaller ones**.

Never compare 2 numbers that have different units of measurement.

A. We convert the day into hours: 1 day = 24 hours
And because 24 hours > 20 hours, 1 day is longer than 20 hours.
So the answer is false

B. We convert months in weeks:
1 month = 4 weeks (we'll always refer to a month as having 4 weeks only)
2 months = 8 weeks
Because 3 weeks < 8 weeks, 3 weeks make a period shorter than 2 months.
The answer is true.

C. We convert weeks into days
1 week = 7 days
2 weeks = 14 days
3 weeks = 21 days
Because 18 days < 21 days, 18 days make a period shorter than 3 weeks.
The answer is false.

DT01-036. Jack was born in 2005. He has two brothers and one sister. Brian was born in 2007, Craig in 2010, and Diane in 2000. Who is the youngest and who is the oldest?

The students have to remember that the youngest guy will always have the greatest year of birth. They can remember that by comparing their years of birth with the one of a baby born this year.

Write again the years in a clearer form:

Jack - 2005
Brian - 2007
Craig - 2010
Diane – 2000

The greatest year of birth is 2010 so Craig is the youngest.
The smallest year of birth is 2000 so Diane must be the oldest.

DT01-037. Jack's brother is exactly 3 years old. How many months old is he?

DT01-038. The soccer season lasted 5 weeks. How many days long was the season?

DT01-039. It takes 40 hours for Dylan's sailboat to get from Port Huron to Mackinac Island. The Fudge Festival will start in exactly 2 days. Will Dylan have enough time to get there?

Remember! To compare different units of times, convert the greater unit into the smaller one.

DT01-040. The first pilgrims moved to America in 1620. Christopher Columbus arrived there in 1492. Who got there first?

DT01-041. John went in a 3 month vacation to Hawaii. He said he stayed there 9 weeks. Was he right?

DT01-042. Which of the following statements are true?
A. One year has 300 days.
B. 2 years have 24 months
C. 2 years have 100 weeks

DT01-043. Because of the storm, Sonia had to stay in the airport 50 hours. Was that more or less than 2 days?

DT01-044. Brian spent 2 months last summer at his grandparents' house in Upper Peninsula. He was there in July and August. How many days did he spend there?

Level 2

The problems in Level 2 are almost the same as in Level 1. The calculations are a little bit different. We deal now with comparison between dates involving not only years, but months and days as well. The students are asked to calculate dates and times in the future or in the past.

DT02-045. Steve was born on November 25, 2005. Today is October 10, 2012. How old is Steve?

The easiest way to solve these problems and make sure the students won't get confused is to write down the age at every birthday:

November 25, 2006 - Steve is 1 year old
November 25, 2007 - Steve is 2 years old
November 25, 2008 - Steve is 3 years old
November 25, 2009 - Steve is 4 years old
November 25, 2010 - Steve is 5 years old
November 25, 2011 - Steve is 6 years old
November 25, 2012 - Steve is 7 years old   -Hey, today is October 10, it's not November 25, 2012 yet! So Steve is not 7 years old yet.
Steve is 6 years old.

DT02-046. Brian is 8 years old and Tom is 7 years old. What will be the sum of their ages three years later?

Brian is 8. After 3 years, he will be 8+3 = 11 years old.

Tom is 7. After 3 years, he will be 7+3= 10 years old.

The sum of their ages after 3 years will be 11 + 10 = 21 years.

DT03-047. Sydney's birthday is August 8, 2005. Olivia's birthday is June 12, 2005. Selena's birthday is February 19, 2004. Doree's birthday is August 8, 2004. Among the four girls, who is the oldest?

The oldest girl has the earliest birth date. So we should look at Selena and Doree who were born in 2004. Selena was born in February, which comes before August so Selena is the oldest.

So first look at years, then months, and then days. Here's the order of their birthdays (from the youngest to the oldest):

Sydney - August 8, 2005
Olivia - June 12, 2005
Doree - August 8, 2004
Selena - February 19, 2004

DT02-048. Joe's birthday is 3 days after Maya's. This year, Maya's birthday is the third Wednesday in October. What is the date of Joe's birthday?

DT02-049. In 7 minutes, it will be 7:00 PM. What time is it now?

DT02-050. A tornado watch was in effect for the Oakland County from 9:30 PM last night to 3:30 AM this morning. How long did the tornado watch last?

DT02-051. Our neighbors left home for a cruise on Thursday. They returned home 11 days later. What day of the week did they return home?

DT02-052. Today is October 10, 2012. Vlad is 7 years old. How old will he be on October 10, 2020?

DT02-053. The Math workshop starts at 6:00 PM. Today Gene was 12 minutes late to the workshop. What time did Gene come?

DT02-054. Today is Wednesday. Sydney's birthday was 4 days ago. On what day of the week was Sydney's birthday?

Level 3

The students should be now able to count the minutes, hours, days backwards and forward.

DT03-055. Josh visited his grandparents on Wednesday, August 22nd, and invited them to his birthday party on September 5th. What day of the week will the birthday party take place?

The key here is to know that August has 31 days. The simplest (not the fastest though) way to solve this problem is by writing down the days:

August						
Su	Mo	Tu	Wed	Th	Fr	Sa
			22	23	24	25
26	27	28	29	30	31	

September						
Su	Mo	Tu	Wed	Th	Fr	Sa
						1
2	3	4	5			

The other way is by counting the days. We know August had 31 days (the students should count their knuckles if they don't know). There are 9 days from August 22nd until August 31st.

And then there are 5 more days until September 5th.

So 14 days in total - that's exactly 2 weeks. So September 5th is going to be a Wednesday.

DT03-056. A train leaves the train station every 15 minutes. If the 1st train leaves 10:15 A.M., what time will be the 10th train leave?

The student can quickly draw a clock if she thinks it's necessary. Write down all the 10 trains with their time of departure:

1st train - 10:15 AM
2nd train - 10:30 AM
3rd train - 10:45 AM
4th train - 11:00 AM
5th train - 11:15 AM
6th train - 11:30 AM
7th train - 11:45 AM
8th train - 12:00 PM - The afternoon starts here
9th train - 12:15 PM
10th train - 12:30 PM

Answer: The 10 train leave the station at 12:30 PM.

DT03-057. Vlad leaves school at 4 o'clock. He has lunch at school 5 hours before he leaves. What time does he have lunch?

DT03-058. A part of Mrs. Mustola's Friday class schedule didn't come up from the printer. If we know that each class is 45 minutes long, and there is no break between classes, what time does Physical Education class start?
9:00 - Math Centers
??? - Writing
??? - Art
??? - Physical Education

DT03-059. There are 5 trains every day that travel between Detroit and Grand Rapids. The departure times are as follows:

6:00 AM, 8:12 AM, 9:44 AM, 10:45 AM, 3:56 PM

The trip takes 3 hours and 15 minutes. If it is 10 AM now, what will be the earliest time I can get to Grand Rapids?

DT03-060. Trenton takes the bus to school at 8 AM and he returns home with the same bus at 4 PM. He spends 45 minutes in the bus going to school, and 30 minutes coming back from school. He also has 1 hour recess. The rest of the time he stays only in the class. How much time does he spend in the class?

DT03-061. The indoor playground at KidsPlay is open Monday through Friday from 10 AM to 9 PM. It is also open on Saturday from 10 AM to 5 PM. It is closed on Sunday. How many hours a week is the playground open?

DT03-062. These are the first 3 finishers in the Brooksie Half Marathon in 2012:
Alexander West - 1 hour 15 minutes 9 seconds
Shane Logan - 1 hour 13 minutes 15 seconds
Ryan Beck - 1 hour 14 minutes 51 seconds
Who got the gold medal?

DT03-063. Today is 10/10/2012. No item can be sold after the "Sell by" date. Which of the following items can't be sold today?
Cheese - Sell by 12/10/2012
Milk - Sell by 10/12/2012
Butter - Sell by 9/10/2012

DT03-064. When I was 2 my brother had half my age. Now I am 100 years old. How old is my brother?

Week 2 Three Little Birds

LB-065 Last night it snowed all through the night from 9 PM until 6 AM. For the first 4 hours, 3 inches of snow fell every hour. Then it slowed down, and only 2 inches of snow fell every hour. What was the accumulation of snow at 6 AM in the morning?

LB-066 There are twice as many red pencils as blue pencils in a box. If 5 red pencils are removed from the box, the number of red pencils will be the same as the number of blue pencils. How many blue pencils are in the box?

LB-067 Sydney bought a tea kettle and a set of tea cups for $110. If the kettle costs $80 more than the set of cups, how much does the kettle cost?

Week 2 Angry Bird

AB-068 If Greg gave Tom 4 dimes, he would still have 8 more dimes than Tom. If Tom started with 10 dimes, how many dimes did Greg start with?

Week 3

Week 3 Letter to the Parents

We went through the problems given at Noetic Contest 2 years ago. I wanted to have them all covered but we didn't have time for the last 2. Here's where we spent more time:

- I realized the kids have difficulties in dealing with hypothetical situations, the "if" details that sometimes are given in the problems. The problems are really not difficult but the perspective is a little bit different. They just have to get used to them. They don't quite get "If I double my money, I'll have 5 dollars. How much do I have now?", but they don't have any issues with "What is half of 5?" It's amazing how their minds work.

- Fractions. Of course, I didn't expect them to know fractions even though they did an introduction in the first grade. Number Cruncher solved the problem in few seconds using a method that he said he learned in the 1st grade. The method is great, but it only works when the numerator is 1 (1/2, 1/3, etc), and that was the case with this problem. We worked on a different way to solve fractions and I think they got it. We'll talk more about it next week, when we'll do only fractions.

- The kids learned that when they have to calculate the age, given the birth date, the month and date are very important, not just the year (they all gave the wrong answer to a problem of this kind in the test). I am going to ask them a similar question next time to make sure they got it right.

- We discussed about min and max. The kids haven't had exposure to these terms before and they weren't sure what they meant. I think they got it now.

- I has happy the kids recognized the "more or less" problems in the test, and they applied one of the 2 strategies they learned.

As part of the curriculum, we talked about patterns. We started with easy ones and ended up with sequences that involved 2 or 3 operations.

As I promised last week, I showed the kids few interesting things about the Fibonacci series. The kids were fascinated when I showed them how to draw a perfect spiral using Fibonacci numbers.

The Presenter told me a few days ago that they had a first introduction to algebra at school and I was dying to know how they perceived it. So I asked them to give me an example. The Number Cruncher rushed to the white board and wrote the following equation: $12 + x = 23 + 13$. And then he carried on offering us some hints: you have to add the numbers on the right side of the = sign and then subtract 12. The Engineer jumped from his seat right away - "No, you don't need to do anything! No addition, no subtraction. The answer is 24!" We all stared at him in disbelief. "If you get rid of 12 on the both sides of the equal sign, we'll be left with x on one side and 23+1 on the side. So x is 24. " The kids got that immediately and all I had to do was shake the Engineer's hand. You don't get to see very often such a great algebraic thinking on a 2nd grader.

Week 3 Story – Fibonacci Numbers

The Fibonacci sequence was introduced by Leonardo Fibonacci in his 1202 book "Liber Abaci" (The Book of Calculations). It was the first book to describe the Arabic numerals and their major advantages that Fibonacci learned while he lived in North Africa with his father, Guglielmo Bonacci. Leonardo was known as Figlio di Bonacci (Bonacci's son), which became Fibonacci.

The applicability of the sequence was actually discovered by the Indian mathematicians long before that; Fibonacci learned about it from some great Arab mathematicians of the time and used it as an example of the use of Arabic numerals in his book.

The first numerals in the sequence are 1, 1, (or 0, 1, 1) and each subsequent number is the sum of the previous two:

1, 1, 2, 3, 5, 8, 13, 21, 34 ...

If you use these numbers as sides for squares and attach the squares one to another, you get a perfect spiral:

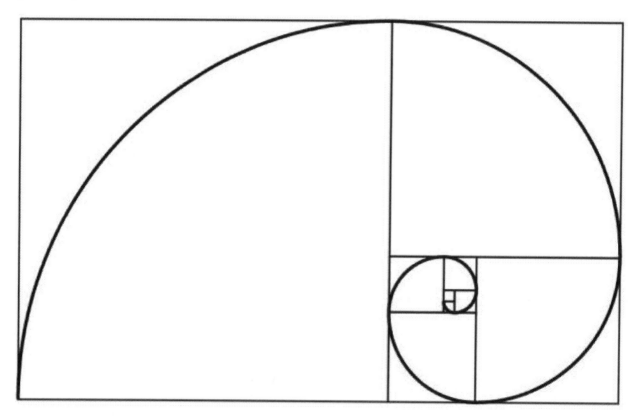

The sequence can be found very often in nature:
- The arrangement of a pinecone
- The flowering of artichoke, sunflower, chamomile
- The fruitlets of a pineapple
- The spiral of shells

Aloe:

Pinecone:

Shell:

Rose:

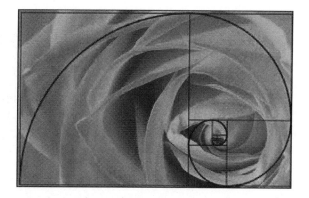

Here's a nice video about the famous sequence:

https://www.youtube.com/watch?v=PotLbl5LrJ8

Week 3 Curriculum – Patterns

Level 1

A sequence is a set of things that are in order and follow a particular rule. That rule is also called **pattern**. There are a lot of different rules/patterns. In Level 1 we start with a very basic one – add or subtract a number to generate the following number.

PT01-069. Continue the following sequence:

1, 5, 9, 13, ___, ___

- Determine if the order of numbers is ascending (getting larger in value) or descending (becoming smaller in value).
- Find the pattern (the difference between numbers that are next to each other).
- Use the pattern to find the next number.

In this case the rule is add 4 because the difference between the second and the first number is 4. We can see that the rule is also true for the third and the fourth number. We will apply the same rule to find the fifth and the sixth numbers.

1, 5, 9, 13, 17, 21,

Rule: +4

PT01-070. Find the pattern and continue the following sequence:

88, 80, 72, ___, ___,

In this case the numbers are descending so the rule must involve subtractions. The difference between the first and the second number is 8, and we can see that the rule holds true for the third number as well.

88, 80, 72, 64, 48
Rule: - 8

Sometimes the rule is not applied to every number. Here's an example:

PT01-071. Find the pattern and continue the following sequence:

2, 2, 2, 11, 11, 11, 20, 20, 20, ___, ___, ___, ___

In this case the rule is applied to every third number. The difference between the 4th number and the 3rd is 9, and it is the same with the difference between the 7th and the 6th.

2, 2, 2, 11, 11, 11, 20, 20, 20, 29, 29, 29, 38
Rule: Add 9 to every third number.

PT01-072. Continue the sequence:
45, 56, 67, ___, ___

PT01-073. Continue the sequence:
89, 81, 73, ___, ___

PT01-074. Continue the sequence:
88, 88, 79, 79, 70, ___, ___

PT01-075. Continue the sequence:
34, 45, 56, ___, ___

PT01-076. Continue the sequence:
121, 102, 83, ___, ___

PT01-077. Continue the sequence:
4, 4, 22, 22, 40, ___, ___

PT01-078. Continue the sequence:
84, 69, 44, ___, ___

Level 2

The problems in the second level deal mostly with 2 steps rules. The first rule is applied to the first number in the sequence and the second rule is applied to the second. Then the first rule kicks in again and so on. Here's an example:

PT02-079. Continue the following sequence:

5, 6, 10, 11, 15, 16, 20, 21, 25, ___, ___

- Find the rule required to generate the second number: + 1 in this case
- Check if the rule is applicable for the third number. It is not in this case. Then find the rule required to generate the third number: + 4
- Check if any of the 2 rules applies to the 4th number. Rule 1 is used to generate the 4th number and then Rule 2 is used to generate the 5th number.
- The pattern is "add 1 and then add 4". Use the pattern to find the next number.

5, 6, 10, 11, 15, 16, 20, 21, 25, 26, 30

Rule: Add 1 and then add 4

Different operations can be used in the same patterns. Here's an example.

PT02-080. Find the pattern and continue the following sequence:

4, 9, 7, 12, 10, ___, ___,

In this case the numbers are neither descending nor ascending. So there must be different operations used in the pattern.

Rule 1 is "add 5": 4 + 5 = 9
Rule 2 is "subtract 2": 9 – 2 = 7
Rule 1 is applied to the 4th number: 7 + 5 = 12
Rule 2 is applied to the 5th number: 12 – 2 = 10

4, 9, 7, 12, 10, 15, 13

Rule: Add 5 and then subtract 2

In level 1 we used patterns there were applied to every third number. Here's an example where the pattern is applied to every second and third number:

PT02-081. Find the pattern and continue the following sequence:

9, 9, 8, 7, 7, 6, 5, 5, 4, __, __

This pattern can be determined even visually – 2 nines, 1 eight, 2 sevens, 1 six, 2 fives, 1 four, so we must have 2 threes following. The mathematical pattern is "subtract 1 from every second and third number".

9, 9, 8, 7, 7, 6, 5, 5, 4, 3, 3
Rule: Subtract 1 from every second and third number.

PT02-082. Continue the sequence:
18, 18, 16, 14, 14, 12, 10, 10, 8, __, __

PT02-083. Continue the sequence:
6, 18, 12, 24, 18, 30, 24, 36, 30, ___, ___

PT02-084. Continue the sequence:
24, 23, 20, 19, 16, 15, 12, 11, 8, ___, ___

PT02-085. Continue the sequence:
24, 29, 27, 32, 30, ___, ___

PT02-086. Continue the sequence:
121, 131, 135, 145, 149, ___, ___

PT02-087. Continue the sequence:
17, 22, 29, 34, 41, ___, ___

PT02-088. Continue the sequence:
94, 99, 89, 94, 84, ___, ___

Level 3

The patterns in the third level are a little bit more complex. They may involve the previous members of the sequence to generate the following number. Few examples of patterns:

- Sum of the previous 2 or 3 numbers

- 2 different operations involving more of the previous numbers

Let's work on some examples:

PT03-089. Continue the following sequence:

5, 6, 11, 17, 28, ___, ___

- We can see that adding or subtracting a number doesn't really work here. Second number: +1, third number: +5, fourth number: +6, fifth number: +11. This can't be a pattern.
- We can notice that each member of the sequence is generated by adding the previous 2 members (a modified version of Fibonacci numbers)
- Verify the pattern: 11 = 5 + 6, 17 = 6 + 11, 28 = 11 + 17
- Continue the sequence: 17 + 28 = 45, 28 + 45 = 73

5, 6, 11, 17, 28, 45, 73

Rule: Sum of the previous 2 numbers

PT03-090. Find the pattern and continue the following sequence:

2, 2, 4, 8, 14, 26, ___, ___,

Adding the previous 2 numbers seems to work for the first 3 numbers but then the rules does hold true anymore. Adding the previous 3 numbers works in this case:

8 = 2 + 2 + 4
14 = 2 + 4 + 8
26 = 4 + 8 + 14

Generate the following numbers:

8 + 14 + 26 = 48
14 + 26 + 48 = 88
2, 2, 4, 8, 14, 26, 48, 88

Rule: Sum of the previous 3 numbers
There may be more than 1 operations involving the previous numbers

PT03-091. Find the pattern and continue the following sequence:

2, 8, 4, 6, 6, 4, 8, 2, 10, __, __

In this sequence, the 4th number is generated by adding the first 2 and subtracting the third:
6 = 2 + 8 − 4
6 = 8 + 4 − 6
4 = 4 + 6 − 6
8 = 6 + 6 − 4
2 = 6 + 4 − 8
10 = 4 + 8 - 2

Find the following numbers:

$8 + 2 - 10 = 0$
$2 + 10 - 0 = 12$
2, 8, 4, 6, 6, 4, 8, 2, 10, 0, 12

Rule: Add the first 2 numbers and subtract the third.

PT03-092. Continue the sequence:
8, 10, 18, 28, 46, ___, ___

PT03-093. Continue the sequence:
12, 10, 8, 14, 4, 18, 0, ___

PT03-094. Continue the sequence:
2, 4, 6, 12, 22, 40, ___, ___

PT03-095. Continue the sequence:
2, 4, 6, 10, 16, ___, ___

PT03-096. Continue the sequence:
12, 13, 14, 39, 67, ___, ___

PT03-097. Continue the sequence:
3, 9, 5, 7, 7, 5, 9, 3, ___, ___

PT03-098. Continue the sequence:
2, 3, 4, 9, 16, 29, ___, ___

Week 3 Three Little Birds

LB-099. Joe is 3'10" tall. His younger brother, Moe, is 2'4" tall. Their father, Dustin, is as tall as Joe and Moe together. How much taller is Dustin than Joe?

LB-100. Jack has 2 math worksheets due tomorrow. There are 13 problems in one worksheet and he completed 5 of them. There are 15 problems in the other worksheet and he completed 8 of them. How many math problems does Jack have left to do altogether?

LB-101. Two 2nd grade classes went on a field trip to Dinosaur Hill. Each class had 11 students, 1 teacher, 1 para-professional, and 1 parent. How many people went on a field trip?

Week 3 Angry Bird

AB-102. Nick had an equal number of pennies, nickels and dimes. Robert has twice as many nickels as Nick. He also has 4 more pennies and 3 more dimes than Nick has. Robert has 9 pennies. How much money does Robert have in total?

Week 4

Week 4 Letter to the Parents

I tried to keep a relaxed pace for this session because it was the last one before the Noetic Math Fall Contest. We did the problems in the 2011 Fall contest and then we talked and watched a movie about Terence Tao, a child prodigy and one of the best mathematicians in the world.

Then we talked about the contest. There were few things that wanted the kids to keep in mind

It's essential for them to stay focused. I'll even write that on the board to remind them when they raise their eyes from the paper.

Once they get their papers, they will be on their own; I won't answer any questions and give them any clues. However, I will clarify for them the meaning of any words that they might not be familiar with.

They will have 45 minutes to finish the test. That's more than enough. I'm sure they will finish before that. I suggested them not to leave right away after they finish. They should take their time and check and double check every problem. There is no rush. In 80% of the cases, the students find errors during the checks if they are thorough with that. I wish I could have a penny for every time that happened to me. I don't want them to be in the situation to realize they made a mistake after they handed the paper.

Few things about "contest etiquette": I asked the kids to show respect to everyone else in the room by being quiet and not engaging their neighbors in any other kind of activities or discussions. Everyone is in an intense thinking process and there should not be any distractions. All the requests should be addressed to me by raising their hands. I made a special request to the Number Cruncher to keep this rule in mind.

I'm sure the kids will do well as long as they follow the rules above. I've been telling them for few weeks about the FFFCDC rule and I think they got it: Focus, Focus, Focus, Check and Double Check.

As for me, I am very excited and I consider myself lucky to play a small part in their first math contest of their lives. This is just the beginning; they will have hundreds coming up, but the first one will always be The First.

We also worked on the Fractions modules. We started with simple problems in Level 1, where the kids had to write the parts out of the whole, we carried on with the second level, where they learned the "Sticky Method" to solve any fraction problems, and we finished with Level 3 problems, where the fractions were combined with other operations. We also talked about the 2 parts of a fraction – Numerator and Nominator.

Week 4 Story – Terence Tao

Terence Tao was an exceptionally gifted kid, a child prodigy, and now is Professor of Mathematics at UCLA (University of California, Los Angeles). He became professor when he was 24, the youngest person ever appointed to that rank by the institution.

He was born in Australia in Adelaide, Australia on July 17th 1975.

He learned the numbers and letters by watching Sesame Street.

When he was only 2 years old, he was trying to teach 5 year old kids additions and subtractions.

He scored 760 on the SAT math section when he was 8.

He was the youngest participant in the **International Mathematical Olympiad**. He won bronze when he was 10, silver at 11 and gold at the age of 12.

He got his **bachelor and master degree at the age of 16, and PhD at the age of 20** (Princeton University).

He still lives now in Los Angeles along with his wife and their son and daughter. His wife, Laura, is an engineer at **NASA's Jet Propulsion Laboratory**.

We'll talk about how Terry deals with frustrations when he's not able to solve a problem, and what he thinks about working in a team.

We'll also watch one or two short movies, depending on how much time we have.

https://www.youtube.com/watch?v=xKWm-zPHnrw

https://www.youtube.com/watch?v=p6ZUeQv2yFQ

Week 4 Curriculum - Fractions

Level 1

In the first level we focus on dividing the whole in equal parts and identifying the fractions. We'll also discuss about ordering the fractions and naming the 2 elements of a fraction: the numerator (the number above the line) and denominator (the number underneath the line).

FR1-103 Write the correct fraction for each of the shaded part of the following shapes:

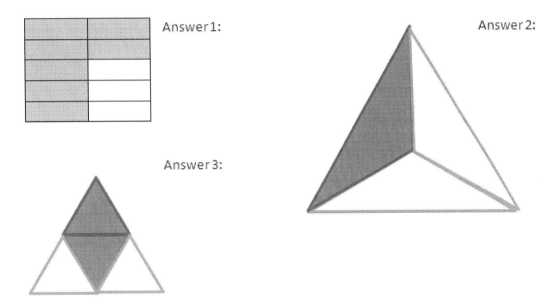

The students will have to count the total number of equal parts and then to determine how many of them are shaded. The total number will go under the line and the number of shaded parts will go above the line.

$$Fraction = \frac{Number\ of\ Shaded\ Parts}{Total\ Number\ of\ Equal\ Parts}$$

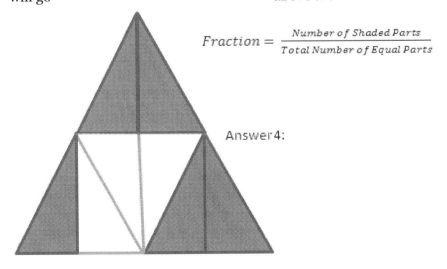

Answer 4:

FR1-104 Write > or < to compare the following fractions:

49

$\frac{1}{2}\ \bigcirc\ \frac{1}{4}$ $\qquad$ $\frac{1}{3}\ \bigcirc\ \frac{1}{5}$

$\frac{1}{5}\ \bigcirc\ \frac{1}{8}$ $\qquad$ $\frac{1}{6}\ \bigcirc\ \frac{1}{5}$

When comparing fractions, if the **numerators** are equal, the fraction with the smaller **denominator** has the greater value. For example, 1/2 is greater than 1/8, 3/5 is greater than 3/7.

$$Fraction = \frac{Numerator}{Denominator}$$

A good mnemonic to remember which one is above and which one is underneath the line is **Nice Dogs**. Nice (Numerator) comes before (or above) Dogs (Denominator). Also, Denominator starts with D, just like Down.

FR1-105 Arrange the fractions in order, beginning with the smallest:

$\frac{1}{8}$ $\qquad$ $\frac{1}{2}$ $\qquad$ $\frac{1}{9}$ $\qquad$ $\frac{1}{4}$ $\qquad$ $\frac{1}{12}$

FR1-106 Compare the following fractions:

3/5 and 3/7; 2/7 and 2/3; 1/4 and 1/2; 5/7 and 5/9

FR1-107 Arrange the fractions in order, beginning with the smallest:

2/3   2/5   2/11   2/7   2/4

FR1-108 Josh won today a math contest and his mom doubled his allowance to $6 a week. What was his allowance last week?

FR1-109 Arrange the fractions in order, beginning with the greatest:

5/6   5/11   5/7   5/9   5/12

FR1-110 Compare the following fractions:

4/7 and 4/5; 5/9 and 5/7; 7/8 and 7/11

FR1-111 Maria got 10 apples from her grandma. She gave half of them to her friend, Ann. How many apples did Ann get?

FR1-112 John has 48 black and white Lego pieces. Half of them are black. How many white Lego pieces does he have?

Level 2

In the first level the students got a glimpse of some word problems with fractions. They only had to find the half of a number. In the second level we start working on more complicated word problems. The students will have to "translate" the words into fractions and use the knowledge acquired in Level 1 to solve the problems.

FR2-113 Ron built a Lego house using 24 red and yellow pieces. One fourth of the Lego pieces were red. How many where yellow?

The most straightforward method to solve this kind of problems is again to make a drawing. We will draw 24 sticks representing the Lego pieces. I call it the "Sticky Method" (because we draw sticks)

Step 1:

| | | | | | | | | | | | | | | | | | | | | | | | |

We need to find out what is 1/4 of the pieces. We will divide the total number of pieces in groups of 4:

Step 2:

| | | | │ | | | | │ | | | | │ | | | | │ | | | | │ | | | |

Then we mark just one piece in each group, because only one fourth of the pieces are red:

Step 3:

Ⓘ | | | │Ⓘ | | | │Ⓘ | | | │Ⓘ | | | │Ⓘ | | | │Ⓘ | | |

And then we just have to count the marked pieces:

1/4 of the total of 24 pieces are red and that is 6. We need to find the number of the yellow pieces though.

Answer:

There are 24 − 6 = 18 yellow pieces of Lego in Ron's house

The same method can be used for more complex problems, as we will see in Level 3

FR2-114 Alex gave away a third of his collection of baseball cards and remained with 12. How many cards did he use to have?

Once again, start drawing:

The total number of cards (we don't know how many):

Alex gives a third (1/3) away and remains with 12:

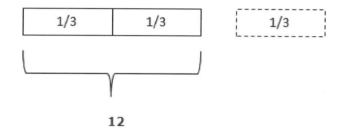

So 2 thirds are 12 cards. One third would be 6 cards:

6

Alex used to have 18 cards:

6	6	6

FR2-115 Briana had $18. She spent a third of her money on a movie ticket and a half of the money for a sandwich. How much did she have left?

Use the Sticky Method if you don't know what one third (1/3) of $18 is. But you should really know what one half of 18 is. That's been done in the class at school.

Movie Ticket – 1/3 of $18 is $6

Sandwich – 1/2 of $18 is $9

Total spent: 9+6 = $15

Money left: 18 – 15 = $3

FR2-116 Min returned 1/5 of the books that he checked out from the public library last week. He is planning to read the remaining 8 books by the end of the week. How many books did he check out?

FR2-117 Vlad has a collection of 30 stones. 1/5 of them are quartz minerals, 1/6 of them are lava stones, and the rest of them are Petoskey stones. How many Petoskey stones does Vlad have?

FR2-118 Stony Creek Farm has 18 bunnies. 1/6 of them are white and the rest of them are black. How many black bunnies are there?

FR2-119 Gene's mom got back from the farmer's market with 24 fruits. 1/2 of them were apples, 1/4 were peaches, 1/6 of them were plums. The rest of the fruits were pears. How many pears did she buy?

FR2-120 After John gave Sydney 1/4 of his stamps collection, he still had 21 stamps left. How many stamps did John have initially?

FR2-121 There are 24 students in Mrs. Mustola class. 1/3 of them are boys. How many girls are there?

FR2-122 Trenton uses a bucket with 100 tennis balls in his daily training. Today he's going to practice his serve with 1/4 of the ball and his backhand shot with 1/5 of the balls. He'll use the rest of the balls to practice his forehand shot. How many balls will he use for his forehand?

Level 3

In the third level the fractions are getting more complicated. The numerator can now be any number, not necessarily 1. The good news is that the students can use the same method they learned in Level 2 (the Sticky Method). The problems may deal now with more than one fraction.

FR3-123 Josh built a Lego car using 24 red and yellow pieces. Five eights of the Lego pieces were red. How many red pieces did Josh use? How many blue?

You can see that the greater the total number is, the longer it takes to draw the sticks. Fortunately, the 2nd grade students will never be required to find 23/112 from 336.

Step 1:

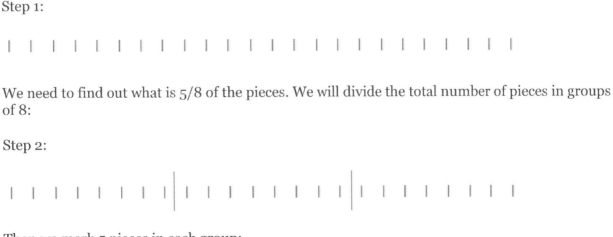

We need to find out what is 5/8 of the pieces. We will divide the total number of pieces in groups of 8:

Step 2:

Then we mark 5 pieces in each group:

Step 3:

OOOOO | | | | OOOOO | | | | OOOOO | | | |

And then we just have to count the marked pieces:

5/8 of the total of 24 pieces are red and that is 5 + 5 + 5 = 15.

Answer:

There are 15 red pieces of Lego in Josh's car and 24 – 15 = 9 yellow pieces.

FR3-124 Cole has a collection of 18 shiny Ninjagos. He gave one third of them to Vlad. Then he gave one half of the remaining ones to Gene. How many Ninjagos did Cole have left?

Initial count: 18

He gives 1/3 away. That's 6 (you can use the Sticky Method or Trial and Error)

He has now 18 – 6 = 12

He gives away again 1/2 of the remaining ones – that 1/2 of 12 = 6

Answer:

He has now 12 – 6 = 6 Ninjagos

FR3-125. Joe has $25 to spend at the fair. He gives two fifths of his money to his friend who didn't have any, and then he spent two thirds of the remaining money on games. After that he wanted to eat a hamburger that cost $4.99. Does he have enough money to buy the hamburger?

FR3-126. Vlad has just started a collection of Discovery magazines. He collected 6 magazines – that's only 2/5 of his neighbor's collection. How many magazines does his neighbor have?

FR3-127. There are 32 students in Mrs. Mustola's class. Three fourths of them like to read in the Free Choice hour. Three fourths of the remaining students like to draw. The rest of the students paint. How many students paint?

FR3-128. Sydney has 18 Magic Tree House books. She wants to trade 5/6 of them for some Ramona books. How many Magic Tree House books will she have left?

FR3-129. Gene's soccer practice is 1 hour and a half. He spends 1/3 of that for warm-up, 1/2 of the remaining time for speed drills. He practices his goal shot for the rest of the time. He shots 2 times every minute. How many shots does he do?

FR3-130. One large pizza usually feeds 4 people. How many people will 2 and a half pizzas feed?

FR3-131. A sack of oat will feed 4 horses. How many horses will two and a half sacks feed?

FR3-132. Dan's grandma usually uses two and half cups of flour to bake 30 cookies. But today she only wants to bake 15 cookies. How much flour would she need?

Week 4 Three Little Birds

LB-133. Dan is in the 3rd grade now and he would like to donate his Kindergarten books. He gives 3/7 of his books to his cousin, and a half of the remaining ones to his neighbor. He still has 6 remaining books and he's thinking to donate them to the Public Library. How many books did Dan initially have?

LB-134. Trenton and Gene collect postage stamps. Trenton has 21 stamps and gave Gene 6 stamps to have both the same number. How many did Gene have initially?

LB-135. The sum of 2 numbers is 12. Their difference is 10. What is the largest number?

Week 4 Angry Bird

AB-136. A large loaf of bread will last two and a half days for Pete and his parents. How long will the loaf last for the parents when Pete goes in summer camp (presuming that all 3 of them eat the same quantity of bread)?

Week 5

Week 5 Letter to the Parents

We couldn't get a study room anywhere in the Public Library this time so we all sat at one table in the common study area. I was actually about to cancel the meeting but Number Cruncher and Presenter (who got busy with a Sudoku book while waiting for the other 2 colleagues) asked me not to.

We started to focus on the Continental Math League Contest that's coming up in January. I thought of changing a little bit the format of the session, so I gave the kids a quick test in the beginning. I let them work on the problems 10-15 minutes, and then we discussed about their solutions. This approach gives the kids the opportunity to work by themselves on problems, without any help. They asked questions, but I told them to use their own judgment to solve the problems. Another advantage is that the test mimics the real contest, so the kids get used with that too. The test had 3 problems. They solved correctly 2 of them, but they all gave the wrong answer to the third one. I don't know how they even managed to come up with 4 different answers :). We spent more time on that problem to get it clarified and then we went through more problems that were given in the past at Continental Math League Contests.

We decided to have the first Continental Math contest on Saturday, 1/19. It will be in the morning; I still have to confirm the room reservation. I'll send another email tomorrow once I know the time for sure. This contest is going to be the first in a series of 3. Unlike Noetic Math Contest, the medals and certificates will be awarded only after the last contest. The score will be cumulative. The first 2 scorers will get medals.

As you know, I initiated a so called "Angry Bird" contest, with one single challenge problem, where the kids can get a price on the spot if they are able to solve it. None of them have been able to solve it yet. They get so eager to see the Angry Bird each time we meet, hoping that they could get the price. We also have the "Three Little Birds" contest, where the kids have to solve 3 problems each time. They accumulate points based on how many problems they solve correctly. The first student who gets to 12 points will also get a price. They get very excited about that too. I'll send you the standings every week. All I want to do is to awake their competitive spirit, something that the public schools are not very willing to promote nowadays.

We also worked on Ordered Lists problems. The Engineer was so involved in solving all the practice problems that he didn't even notice when we moved to the last part of the session, where we discussed about Gauss and arithmetic series. I asked them how they would calculate the sum of all the numbers from 1 to 100. To my surprise none of the kids tried the hard way; they suspected that there had to be a trick. To my even bigger surprise, Number Cruncher realized that by adding 1 to 99, then 2 to 98, 3 to 97, he always got 100. So the problem can be reduced to summing up 100 several times. He wasn't sure how many times, but he came up with few guesses, one of which was correct! He was very close to the solution that Gauss found when he was 10 years old. I told the kids the story and then we watched a movie about that.

Week 5 Story - Carl Friedrich Gauss

Date of Birth: 4/30/1777
Date of Death: 2/23/1855
Birthplace: Braunschweig

Gauss contributed so much to mathematics that he is sometimes referred to as the Prince of Mathematics. He was referring to math as the "Queen of all the Sciences."

Gauss's mathematical genius is undeniable. He contributed significantly to many fields, including number theory, statistics (the famous Gaussian distribution), analysis, differential geometry, geodesy, geophysics, electrostatics, astronomy and optics. But his favorite by far was mathematics.

There are many stories about Gauss. From some sources, he corrected his father's financial calculations when he was 3 years old. The most famous story comes from his days in the elementary school.

His teacher, J. G. Buttner, gave the students a list of numbers to add together as a means of "busy work." He just needed some time for himself and he thought of keeping the kids busy for a while. He asked the students to add all of the numbers from 1 to 100 together and get a final answer. To the amazement of his teacher and his classmates, Gauss was able to perform this in seconds by using the "trick" below.

1 + 100 = 101, 2 + 99 = 101, 3 + 98 = 101, and so on... Because there are 50 "pairs" that add to 101, the final sum should be 50 x 101 = 5050.

Here's the movie about this story:

http://www.youtube.com/watch?v=arf8wDP_MJE

Week 5 Curriculum – Ordered Lists

Level 1

In the first level the students will have to order values that are known beforehand. This is really not complicated at all, but it is a starting point. To make the things a little bit more complicated, we use sums and differences instead of plain numbers. The students will also practice their knowledge about median and modal.

OL01-137. Put the following sums in ascending order: 12+5, 8+7, 9+7, 10+3

12+5=17; 8+7=15; 9+7=16; 10+3=13

We'll start using tables like the one below for this kind of problems. They may not be necessary for the problems at this level, but they will become useful when the difficulty increases in the next levels.

1st	2nd	3rd	4th
13	15	16	17

Ascending Order: form small to big numbers
Descending Order: form big to small numbers

Solve all the number sentences and then write the lowest number in 1st box for ascending order (for descending order, write the greatest number in the 1st box). Then write the next number in the second box and so on.

OL01-138. Put the following sums and differences in descending order: 24+17, 23+19, 19+34, 15+37, 67-29

24+17=41, 23+19=42, 19+34=53, 15+37=52, 67-29=38

1st	2nd	3rd	4th	5th
53	52	42	41	38

OL01-139. What is the median value of the following set of numbers: 34+17, 33+19, 29+34, 25+37, 77-29?

34+17=51, 33+19=52, 29+34=63, 25+37=62, 77-29=48

1st	2nd	3rd	4th	5th
53	52		41	38

Median – The middle value of the ordered set of numbers

The numbers have to be ordered first and then the middle value will be selected.
The middle value is 42.

OL01-140. What is the median value and the modal in the following set of numbers: 18+7, 12+6, 1+17, 6+5, 9+13, 13+8, 14+9?

18+7=25, 12+6=18, 1+17=18, 6+5=11, 9+13=22, 13+8=21, 14+9=23

1st	2nd	3rd	4th	5th	6th	7th
11	18	18		22	23	25

Modal – The most frequent value in a set of numbers (the most popular number)
The median is 21 and the modal is 18.

OL01-141. Put the following sums in ascending order: 12+14, 18+17, 19+27, 28+3

OL01-142. Put the following sums in descending order: 37+15, 48+17, 39+28, 27+15, 56-17

OL01-143. What is the median value of the following set of numbers: 47, 59, 23, 51, 76?

OL01-144. What is the median value and the modal in the following set of numbers: 22-5, 11+6, 7+5, 6+5, 19+13, 13+8, 14+9?

OL01-145. What is the median value and the modal in the following set of numbers: 12+4, 22-6, 22-11, 6+5, 9+2, 13-8, 14-9?

OL01-146. What is the median value and the modal in the following set of numbers: 18+3, 12+7, 24 -5, 6+6, 9+14, 23-8, 14+9?

Level 2

In the second level we deal with lists that are arranged in a more complicated fashion. The problems offer a lot of details about how the elements of the lists are ordered with respect to one another, and ask for the overall order in the lists.

OL02-147. Jessica has three shirts: one pink, one blue and one green. She arranged them in three drawers. She didn't place the pink shirt in the top drawer; she placed the green shirt in the bottom drawer. She never places the blue shirt in the middle drawer. What shirt did Jessica place in the top drawer?

Any of the 3 shirts can be placed in any of the drawers:

Pink	Blue	Green
Pink	Blue	Green
Pink	Blue	Green

Then we read the facts:
- the pink shirt was not placed in the top drawer – cross out Pink from the top drawer
- the blue shirt was not placed in the middle drawer – cross out Blue from the middle drawer
- the green shirt was placed in the bottom drawer – Cross out Pink and Blue from the bottom drawer. Since the green short was placed in the bottom drawer, we can cross it out from the top and middle drawers

~~Pink~~	Blue	~~Green~~
Pink	~~Blue~~	~~Green~~
~~Pink~~	~~Blue~~	Green

We can now see that the Blue short was placed in the top drawer, the Pink short was placed in the middle drawer, and the Green short – in the bottom drawer.

OL02-148. Mike, Jack and Aaron decided to wear 3 different colors – red, white and blue. Mike likes blue. Jack never wears white. Who wears red?

Mike likes blue – cross out Red and White on Mike's row.
We know for sure that Mike wears blue – cross out Blue on Jack and Aaron's rows.

Mike	~~Red~~	~~White~~	Blue
Jack	Red	White	~~Blue~~
Aaron	Red	White	~~Blue~~

Jack never wears white – cross out white on Jack's line.

Mike	~~Red~~	~~White~~	Blue
Jack	Red	~~White~~	~~Blue~~
Aaron	Red	White	~~Blue~~

So we can see now that the only color that Jack can wear is Red. That answers the problem.

OL02-149. Mike has 5 shirts: 2 yellow and 3 blue. He arranges them in 3 drawers:
1 yellow shirt in the bottom drawer
1 yellow shirt in the middle drawer
Every shirt in the middle drawer is yellow
There are no blue shirts in the bottom drawer
How many shirts are in the top drawer?

OL02-150. Jack, Don, and Mike are three penguins who like to go fishing together. They walk one by one in line. Don and Mike never like to end the line. Jack never likes to lead. Don feels cold most of the time and prefers to walk in the middle, to avoid the wind. Who is leading the group?

OL02-151 Vlad's toy train has 5 cars: white, blue, yellow, green, and red. There are 2 cars in front of the yellow car, and 3 cars in front of the green car. The red car is the caboose. The white car is not in front of the train. What car do you think Vlad will place in front?

OL02-152 Sydney, Daria, and Mary stand in line at the ice-cream shop. Sydney is not the first. Mary is the last in line. Daria is not in the middle. Who is going to get ice-cream first?

OL02-153 Jack, Marvin, and Min stand in line to get on the bus. Jack always waits until everyone else got on the bus. Marvin doesn't like to be the first, and Min doesn't like to stand in the middle. In what order do they get on the bus?

OL02-154 A group of kids stand in line in the ice-cream store. Mary is third in line counting from the beginning of the line and fourth counting from the end of the line. How many kids are in line?

OL02-155 Trenton has 5 shirts: 2 yellow, 2 white, and 1 blue. He arranges them in 3 drawers: There is 1 yellow shirt in the middle drawer and 1 white shirt in the top drawer. There are only 2 shirts in the middle drawer and only 1 shirt in the bottom drawer. The blue shirt is not in the top or middle drawers. What shirts does Trenton have in each drawer?

OL02-156 Sydney, Vlad, Trenton, and Gene are waiting in line at the library to check out their books. The boys let Sydney to be the first in line. Gene is behind Trenton and Vlad is not the last in the line. In what order do they stand in line?

Level 3

In the third level we have lists with consistently 4 or more members that are arranged based on certain criteria. Just like in the second level, the problems offer a lot of details about how the elements of the lists are ordered with respect to one another, and ask for the overall order in the lists, or for the position of a particular element.

OL03-157. Four students are lining up for ice cream. Their names are Alex, Briana, Stan, and Calvin. Alex is ahead of Briana, Briana is ahead of Calvin, and Alex is not the first in line. Who is third in line?

We'll solve this kind of problems using the tables introduced in Level 1.

Alex is not the first in line but he's ahead of Briana and Calvin, which means he's the second in line:

1st	2nd	3rd	4th
	Alex	Briana	Calvin

The remaining student, Stan, is first in line but we don't even need this fact anymore. The third in line is Briana and that's the answer.

OL03-158. Min, Eric, Diane and Xing had a race. Eric finished ahead of Xing. Xing didn't finish in last place. Diane finished the second. Who finished in the first place?

We know that Diane is the second and Xing wasn't the last:

1st	2nd	3rd	4th
	Diane		~~Xing~~

So Xing can be on the first or third position. But we also know that Eric finished ahead of Xing, so Xing is the third and Eric is the first:

1st	2nd	3rd	4th
Eric	Diane	Xing	Min

Answer: Eric finished in the first place.

OL03-159. Jack, Tom, Stan and Randy had a race. Stan didn't finish in first or last place. Randy came in second. Who finished in the third position?

Stan didn't finish first or last. He didn't finish the second either because we know that Randy did. So Stan finished the third, and that's the answer.

1st	2nd	3rd	4th
	Randy	Stan	

We don't have enough information to determine who finished in the first and last position (Jack or Tom), but we don't even need to know that.

Answer: Stan finished in the third position.

OL03-160. Linda, Greg, Calvin and John are the only four people standing in a line. John is not standing next to either Linda or Calvin. Calvin is the first one in line. Who is the second person in line?

OL03-161. Twenty children sit in a row watching a carols concert. Leila is the 14th child from one end of the line. Diane is the 16th child from the other end of the line. How many children are between Leila and Diane?

OL03-162. A group of kids stand in line in the ice-cream store. Mary is third in line counting from the beginning of the line and fourth counting from the end of the line. How many kids are in line?

OL03-163. Greg, Jack, Maia and John are all different heights. Greg and Jack are neither the tallest nor the shortest. Maia is shorter than Jack and John. Who is the tallest kid?

OL03-164 Five cars wait at the traffic light, one behind the other. There are 3 cars in front of the yellow car, and 1 car in front of the red car. The blue car is right in front of the traffic light. The white car is not the last. Where is remaining green car?

OL03-165 Mark, Vincent, Cory and TJ are all different heights. Vincent and Cory are neither the tallest nor the shortest. TJ is shorter than Vincent and Mark. In how many ways can we arrange them in the order of their heights?

OL03-166 Olivia, Jen, Sydney and Delilah are the only 4 girls standing in a line. Sydney is not standing next to either Olivia or Jen. Jen is the last in line. In what order do they stand in line?

Week 5 Three Little Birds

LB-167. Vlad goes on bike race. There are 2 water stops during the race where Vlad can stop and fill his water bottle. The distance between the start point and the first water stop is 7 miles. The distance between the first water stop and the finish line is 8 miles. The distance between the second water stop and the finish line is 5 miles. What is the distance between the start line and the second water stop?

LB-168. Find the value of A, if $59 + A = 65 - A$.

LB-169. Vlad has 18 cookies. He eats either 2 cookie or 3 cookies a day.
Question 1: At least how many days will the cookies last?
Question 2: At most how many days will the cookies last?

Week 5 Angry Bird

AB-170. The teacher brings a jar with marbles in the classroom. There are 7 red marbles, 5 yellow marbles and 2 blue marbles in the jar. The teacher blindfolds Gene and asks him to draw marbles from the jar.
1. How many marbles does Gene have to draw to be sure that he draws at least one red marble?
2. How many marbles does Gene have to draw to be sure that he draws at least one blue marble?
3. How many marbles does Gene have to draw to be sure that he draws at least one yellow marble?
4. How many marbles does Gene have to draw to be sure that he draws at least one marble of each color?

Week 6

Week 6 Letter to the Parents

The kids already have 2 contests under their belts! They did very well in the second contest too. They focused all along the test and they didn't ask as many question as in the first one (well, they only had 6 problems this time…). They had 30 minutes to finish the test but I gave them around 40 minutes. The Presenter was the last to finish after 45 minutes or so. They asked a lot of questions about the problem with distances (LB-167 is a similar problem if you want to have an idea). They didn't seem to understand it. It's true, we haven't done any problems of that kind, but I never thought it will present such difficulties for them. We will work more on that type of problems. This test was the first in a series of 3. The first 2 cumulative scores will receive medals.

Our little contest is going to come to a close pretty soon. The Engineer leads the pack with 9 points. If he scores 3 points next time, he will win the contest. But the race is very tight. The Engineer is followed closely by the Presenter with 8 points; the Number Cruncher is on the 3rd place with 7 points, followed by Joy with 6 points. The Engineer and the Presenter scored 2 points (out of 3) in this week's test not because they didn't know how to solve one of the problems, but because they didn't pay enough attention to what the requirement was. We'll see how the next test goes.

I told the kids about Melanie Wood, a great mathematician and the first female to make the make the US team at the International Math Olympiad. We also watched a movie about her.

We worked on multiplication problem this time. Just an introduction, of course. The kids are not required to know the multiplication table at this level.

Week 6 Story - Melanie Wood

Melanie Wood was the first female American to make the U.S. International Mathematical Olympiad Team in 1997.

She was born in Indianapolis, Indiana in 1981. When she was in the 7th grade, her math teacher invited her to be on the school's MathCounts team. She went to the competition without any preparations and won the first place in her city, then in the state of Indiana, and then the 40th in the nation.

In 9th grade, she got very good scores at the USA Math Olympiad and was selected in the International Math Olympiad team of the 32 students. Her role model was Zvezdeline Stankova, who had won two Silver medals in the IMO competitions as a member of the Bulgarian team and had a PhD in mathematics from Harvard.

In 1999, she received generous offers from Harvard, Stanford, and Duke. It was hard decision for her, but she finally chose Duke because their math department was dedicated to undergraduate education and research.

In the "Dove Role Model" promo, she explained what she was working on:

"P orderings are tools that lets you generalize the number theoretic properties of the factorial function from the integers to other rings, so for example I was interested in rings of integers and imaginary quadratic fields and trying to study whether there was a simultaneous p ordering for all primes in those rings."

I showed the video to my group of 2nd graders and they candidly asked me if she spoke English.

More information about Melanie Wood:

http://en.wikipedia.org/wiki/Melanie_Wood

Discovery Magazine (June 2000 Issue)

Book - Count Down: The Race for Beautiful Solutions at the International Mathematical Olympiad

(http://www.amazon.com/Count-Down-Beautiful-International-Mathematical/dp/B0044KN1XU)

Interview: http://www.maa.org/news/melanie-wood-interview.html

http://www.youtube.com/watch?v=pBdPJC9Qw7k

Week 6 Curriculum – Introduction to Multiplication

Level 1

The first level is an introduction to the repeating groups. Multiplication is nothing else than adding something more than once. The kids were introduced in school to the concept of arrays. We build on that concept and work on very basic multiplication word problems. The kids will be encouraged to write the multiplication sentences using the multiplication sign.

IM1-171 Olivia planted 3 rows of tulips. There are 5 tulips in each row. How many tulips did Olivia plant altogether?

3 rows with 5 tulips in each row: 5 + 5 + 5 = 15

IM1-172. John, Adam, Greg and Aaron went fishing. Each of them caught 3 fish. How many fish did they catch altogether?

The 4 boys caught 3 fish each: 3 + 3 + 3 + 3 = 12

IM1-173. Vlad bought 6 Lego figures. Each figure cost $4. How much did Vlad pay altogether?

IM1-174. Sydney bought 5 boxes of cookies. There are 6 cookies in each box. How many cookies did he buy altogether?

IM1-175. Daria prepared 3 pots of tea. She used 6 cubes of sugar for each pot of tea. How many cubes of sugar did she use altogether?

IM1-176. Vlad spent $2 a week for bagels. How much did he spend in 6 weeks?

IM1-177. John bought 9 pieces of rope. Each piece was 3 meters long. How many meters of rope did John buy?

IM1-178. There are 5 roses planted in a row. How many roses are there in 7 rows?

IM1-179. A book costs $10. Mrs. Johns sold 11 copies of the book. How much money did she receive?

IM1-180. David found 5 nests with 7 eggs in each of them. How many eggs did he find?

Level 2

In the second level, the multiplications are combined with other operations. The students are now encouraged to solve the problems without drawing the arrays and to write the number sentence.

IM2-181 Sydney is getting ready to move to a new house and put all her teddy bears in boxes. When she finished, Sydney had 6 boxes of 5 bears, and 1 box of 3 bears. How many bears does Sydney have?

6 boxes of 5 bears and 1 box of 3 bears: 5 + 5 + 5 + 5 + 5 + 5 + 3 = 33

Number Sentence: 6 x 5 + 3 = 33

IM2-182 Silly bands are sold 7 per package. Timothy wants to give one silly band to each of the 25 kids he invited to his birthday party. How many packages of silly bands should he buy?

7 + 7 = 14 – less than 25

7 + 7 + 7 = 21 – less than 25

7 + 7 + 7 + 7 = 28 – more than 25

So Timothy should by 4 packages of silly bands.

Number Sentence: 25 = 4 x 7 - 3

IM2-183 Donna had 17 stickers. She gave three stickers to each of her four friends. How many stickers does she have left?

IM2-184 Gene earns a star for every 6 problems he solves. He solved 45 problems until today. How many stars did Gene earn?

IM2-185 There are 5 pigs and some chickens in the barn. The chickens and the pigs have 30 legs altogether. How many chickens are there in the barn?

IM2-186 There are 5 bicycles and 3 tricycles left in Rochester Bike Store. How many wheels are there altogether?

IM2-187 Gene has 7 dozens of crayons. He gives Trenton 3 dozens. How many crayons does Gene have now?

IM2-188 The pigs in the barn have all 22 eyes. How many legs do they have?

IM2-189 An apple costs $0.25 and a pineapple costs $1.5. Sydney bought 5 apples and 3 pineapples. How much did she pay?

IM2-190 Josh needs 30 paint brushes for a project. He went to Home Depot and found boxes with 8 brushes. How many boxes did he have to buy?

Level 3

In the third level, the multiplications may still be combined with other operations or types of problems, and the degree of complexity is a little higher. The students don't need to know multiplication tables; they will become familiar with the overall understanding of the multiplication concepts.

IM3-191 There are twice as many chickens as pigs in a barn. If 5 chickens are taken out of the barn, the number of chickens will be the same as the number of pigs. How many pigs are in the barn?

There are twice as many chickens as pigs:

Chickens   Pigs
☐☐   ☐

If 5 chickens are taken out of the barn, the number of chickens will be the same as the number of pigs:

So there are 2 groups of 5 chickens and 1 group of 5 pigs.

Answer: There are 5 + 5 = 10 chickens and 5 pigs in the barn

IM3-192 There are 4 students in the reading club. Each student reads 3 books every month. How many books did the students read in a 3 month vacation?

Month 1: Student 1 – **3 books**; Student 2 – **3 books**; Student 3 – **3 books**; Student 4 – **3 books**

Month 2: Student 1 – **3 books**; Student 2 – **3 books**; Student 3 – **3 books**; Student 4 – **3 books**

Month 3: Student 1 – **3 books**; Student 2 – **3 books**; Student 3 – **3 books**; Student 4 – **3 books**

All the students read 3 + 3 + 3 + 3 = 12 books every month

In a 3 month vacation, they read 12 + 12 + 12 = 36 books

Number sentence: 4 x 3 x 3 = 36 books

IM3-193 Vlad brings home 12 pencils every day from Owl's Nest. He arranges them in boxes of 10 pencils each. He does that until he has only boxes with 10 pencils. How many boxes does he have?

IM3-194 There were 58 people at Gene's party. 5 kids came with both their parents and one grandparent, 7 kids came with both parents, and 8 kids came with only one parent. How many kids came alone at the party?

IM3-195 In the Paintcreek Golf Club's parking lot there are golf carts with 6 wheels and 8 wheels. The total number of wheels is 70. The number of 6-wheel carts is the same as the number of 8-wheel carts. How many 6-wheel carts are in the parking lot?

IM3-196 In Mrs. Jones' class there are 5 desks. 4 students sit on every desk and every student has 3 books. How many books are in Mrs. Jones' class?

IM3-197 Two 2nd grade classes went on a field trip to Dinosaur Hill. Each class had 11 students, 1 teacher, 1 para-professional, and 1 parent. How many people went on a field trip?

IM3-198 22 kids showed up at Vlad's birthday party. He had 3 dozens of cookies and wanted to offer each kid 2 cookies. How many more cookies did he need?

IM3-199. Jeff keeps his collection of Ninjago in his room. He has 4 Ninjagos in each of the 5 shelves and 3 other Ninjagos in each of the 4 boxes under his bed. How many Ninjago does Jeff have?

IM3-200. There are 3 times as many pigs as chickens in a barn. There are 42 legs altogether. How many chickens are in the barn?

Week 6 Three Little Birds

LB-201 Sleepy is taller than Doc by as much as Doc is taller than Happy. Sleepy is 3'3" tall and Doc is 2'9" tall. How tall is Happy?

LB-202 John paid for 5 pencils with 4 quarters, 4 dimes, 2 nickels. The following day he needed to buy 10 more pencils for his friend. He only had 3 quarters and 3 dimes. How much more did he need?

LB-203 What number must be added to the sum of 18 and 17 to equal the sum of 15 and 27?

Week 6 Angry Bird

AB_204 Sam likes to raise rabbits in his farm. The difference between the total number of their legs and the total number of their tails is 30. A rabbit eats 2 carrots every day. How many carrots does Sam need to feed all the rabbits for an entire week?

Week 7

Week 7 Letter to the Parents

This time our little contest went really dramatic. I was sure the kids would get very competitive in our little tournament, but I never thought they would get into it so seriously. They are very ambitious and eager to win. Especially the boys. Joy follows them not far behind, but she's rather amused by how fiercely the boys negotiate with me every single point when I grade their papers. She was so funny when she said at one point that this tournament of ours is like an epic drama...But she wasn't very far from the truth. The race is incredibly tight: 10, 10, 10, 8! So about the test...

When I initially checked the Number Cruncher's test, I saw that one answer was wrong. So I gave him 2 points out of 3. But then when I looked at it a second time, I realized that he solved the problem neatly, explaining every step and using the correct strategy, and he even came up with the correct answer written in a corner of the paper. But somehow, some mysterious spells made him to write a final answer that was totally different from any numbers on the test. Even he was puzzled about how he could do that. I gave him the point because he really solved the problem correctly but I warned him that in a "real" contest, that's not going to happen. I stressed again on how important it is to check everything.

Well, but then I got in trouble, because I created a precedent... When I got to the Presenter's paper, he too used a correct logic for the same problem and solved it nicely, but he used other numbers than the ones given in the problem! We had a long discussion about that but he finally admitted that it wouldn't have been fair to get a point for that problem because he didn't have the correct result written anywhere on the paper (as opposed to the Number Cruncher). I'm sure this was a lesson that they will remember and they will check their papers more thoroughly.

We worked on Division problems this time and we also watched the first part of a very interesting documentary about the US team that went to the 47th International Math Olympiad in 2006. It was interesting to watch how the best young mathematicians in the US were getting ready for the tests, and the way they were focusing during the tests. The kids were glued to my laptop's little screen.

We even looked through some problems given last year at International Math Olympiad (just for fun, of course). They read a geometry problem and immediately jumped with questions, and I had to explain them the difference between an incircle and an excircle :) .

Week 7 Story – The International Math Olympiad

The International Mathematical Olympiad (IMO) is the World Championship Mathematics Competition for High School students and is held annually in a different country. The first IMO was held in 1959 in Romania, with 7 countries participating. It has gradually expanded to over 100 countries from 5 continents. The IMO Advisory Board ensures that the competition takes place each year and that each host country observes the regulations and traditions of the IMO.

It was initially founded for eastern European countries participating in the Warsaw Pact, under the Soviet bloc of influence, but eventually other countries participated as well. Because of this eastern origin, the earlier IMOs were hosted only in eastern European countries, and gradually spread to other nations.

Several students, such as Teodor von Burg, Lisa Sauermann and Christian Reiher, have performed exceptionally well on the IMO, scoring multiple gold medals. Others, such as Grigory Margulis, Jean-Christophe Yoccoz, Laurent Lafforgue, Stanislav Smirnov, Terence Tao and Grigori Perelman, have gone on to become notable mathematicians. Several former participants have won awards such as the Fields medal.

The paper consists of six problems, with each problem being worth seven points, the total score thus being 42 points. No calculators are allowed. The examination is held over two consecutive days; the contestants have four-and-a-half hours to solve three problems per day. The problems chosen are from various areas of secondary school mathematics, broadly classifiable as geometry, number theory, algebra, and combinatorics. They require no knowledge of higher mathematics such as calculus and analysis, and solutions are often short and elementary. However, they are usually disguised so as to make the process of finding the solutions difficult.

The selection process for the IMO varies greatly by country. In some countries, especially those in East Asia, the selection process involves several difficult tests of a difficulty comparable to the IMO itself. The Chinese contestants go through a camp, which lasts from March 16 to April 2.

In the USA, possible participants go through a series of easier standalone competitions that gradually increase in difficulty. In the case of the USA, the tests include the American Mathematics Competitions, the American Invitational Mathematics Examination, and the United States of America Mathematical Olympiad, each of which is a competition in its own right. For high scorers on the final competition for the team selection, there also is a summer camp, like that of China.

In Ukraine, for instance, selection tests consist of four Olympiads comparable to the IMO by difficulty and schedule.

In India, the students are subjected to a test called AMTI, region-wise and then some of them are selected for RMO (Regional Mathematics Olympiad). Selected Students are subjected to INMO (Indian National Mathematics Olympiad), from which nationally 35-36 children are selected. They are subjected to a rigorous camp, from which 6 are selected to represent India at IMO. All the exams are rigorous and need a passion and a certain amount of intelligence to pass.

You can watch here a great movie about the US team that went to the 47th International Math Olympiad in 2006:

http://www.youtube.com/watch?v=r-pdFykFotg

Week 7 Curriculum – Introduction to Division

Level 1

The first level is an introduction to the repeating groups. If multiplication is adding something more than once, the division is the reversed process. It is finding the value of the individual parts that add up to a given value. At this level, division involves a lot of trials and errors, since the division and multiplication tables are not yet introduced. The kids will be encouraged to write the division sentences using the division sign.

ID1-205 Olivia packs 12 pounds of flour equally into 4 bags. How many pounds of oat are there in each bag?

🏵 + 🏵 + 🏵 + 🏵 = 12

3 + 3 + 3 + 3 = 12

🏵 = 3 lb. | 12 ÷ 4 = 3 |

ID1-206 28 children lined up in 4 equal rows. How many children were there in each row?

| 28 ÷ 4 = 7 |

ID1-207 Vlad paid $24 for 6 Lego figures. How much was one figure?

ID1-208 Three pieces of rope are of the same length. Their total length is 15 m. How long is each piece of rope?

ID1-209 Sydney arranged 18 roses in 3 bouquets. How many roses were there in each bouquet?

ID1-210 Gene saves $5 a week. He wants to buy a Lego set that costs $40. How many weeks will he need to save enough money?

ID1-211 Vlad, Gene, Sydney and Trenton share a prize of $20 equally. How much money did each of them receive?

ID1-212 Trenton tied 32 pencils into 4 equal bundles. How many pencils were there in each bundle?

ID1-213 Sydney paid $45 for 9 flowers. What was the cost of 1 flower?

ID1-214 David arranged 70 chairs in 10 rows, each row having the same number of chairs. How many chairs were there in a row?

Level 2

In the second level, the divisions are combined with other operations. The concept of remainder is also introduced. Students are now encouraged to solve the problems without drawing, and to always write the number sentences. As in the first lever Trial and Error is still our best friend until we know the division and multiplication facts.

ID2-215 A group of 43 people have to go to the airport in cars with 5 seats each. How many cars do they need?

Add 5 until you get the closest to 43:

```
5 + 5 + 5 + 5 + 5 + 5 + 5 + 5 + 3 = 43
↓   ↓   ↓   ↓   ↓   ↓   ↓   ↓   ↓
1   2   3   4   5   6   7   8   9
```

$43 \div 5 = 8 \text{ Remainder } 3$

They would need 9 cars. The 9th car will only have 3 passengers.

ID2-216 Vlad wants to arrange 27 marbles in boxes. Each box has to have exactly 6 marbles. How many boxes does he need? How many marbles are left over?

Keep on adding 6 until you get the closest to 27:

```
6 + 6 + 6 + 6 + 3 = 27
↓   ↓   ↓   ↓
1   2   3   4
```

$27 \div 6 = 4 \text{ Remainder } 3$

He needs 4 boxes. Since every box has to have exactly 6 marbles, Vlad can't use a box to store only 3 marbles – they will be left over.

✓ **ID2-217** Vlad has 23 candies. He wants to share some of them with Trenton, Sydney and Gene. He keeps 5 for himself and gives each of his friends the same number of candies. How many candies did each of them get?

ID2-218 Trenton has 14 pencils. He wants to arrange them in 3 equal groups. How many pencils are there in each group? Are there any pencils left over?

ID2-219 Gene has a rope which is 32 inches long. He cuts it into pieces of 6 inches long each. How many inches of rope are left over?

ID2-220 Sydney packs 33 cookies in bags, 4 cookies in each bag. How many bags does she need?

ID2-221 If Gene gets straight A's this year, his mother promised him to double his weekly allowance to $5. What is Vlad's current allowance?

ID2-222 Vlad can solve 18 math problems in one hour. How many problems can he solve in 10 minutes?

ID2-223 Trenton has 23 candies. He wants to share some of them with 4 of his friends. He keeps 7 for himself and gives each of his friends the same number of candies. How many candies did each of them get?

ID2-224 A boat can take 5 people at a time from mainland to an island near the shore. Today there are 28 people who want to go to the island. How many trips are required for the boat to take all the people to the island?

Level 3

ID3-225 Vlad brings 5 apples to school, Daria brings 11, Sydney brings 8 and Gene doesn't bring anything. They put all the apples together and divide them equally among themselves. How many apples will each of them get?

Total number of apples: 5 + 11 + 8 = 24 apples
The apples will be divided equally among the 4 friends:

$$24 \div 4 = 6$$

ID3-226 The owner of a flower shop keeps the flowers in 4 vases. There were 7 flowers in the first vase, 4 flowers in the second vase, and 6 flowers in the third vase. The fourth vase has as many flowers as all the other three put together. The first customer buys a bouquet of 3 flowers. But then the owner wants to make more money, so he decides to sell only bouquets of 5 flowers each. After selling some bouquets, she noticed that she didn't have enough flowers to make another bouquet. How many flowers did she have left? How many customers bought flowers?

ID3-227 Vlad has 12 cookies. He eats either 2 cookie or 3 cookies a day.
Question 1: At least how many days will the cookies last?
Question 2: At most how many days will the cookies last?

ID3-228 There are 4 chickens and some cows in the barn. The chickens and the cows have 40 legs altogether. How many cows are there in the barn?

ID3-229 There are 3 chickens and some pigs in the barn. The chickens and the pigs have 30 legs altogether. How many pigs are there in the barn?

ID3-230 The pigs in the barn have all 32 legs. How many eyes do they have?

ID3-231 There are 24 students in Mrs. Mustola's class. Half of them went to the Math Pentathlon. One third of the students who participated in the Math Pentathlon competition won medals. How many student got medals?

ID3-232 In Mrs. Johns' class there are 21 students. After she pairs each boy with a girl for chess games, she realizes that half of the boys don't have pairs. How many boys are in the class?

ID3-233 Daria has 24 problems to solve. She can solve either 2 problems or 3 problems a day.
Question 1: At least how many days will Daria need to solve all the problems?
Question 2: At most how many days will Daria need to solve all the problems?

ID3-234 There is an equal number of chickens and rabbits in a barn. The total number of legs is 36. The farmer has only 24 carrots left to feed the rabbits. If a rabbit eats 2 carrots every day, how many days will the carrots last?

Week 7 Three Little Birds

LB-235 There are 17 students in the class. Sydney did a survey and she found out that 10 students like math and 12 students like reading. How many students like both math and reading?

LB-236 Vlad's grandma has hens and pigs in her small farm. There are 12 hens and a total of 72 legs. How many pigs does Grandma have?

LB-237 In Mrs. Johns' class there are 22 students. After she pairs each boy with a girl for a dance recital, she will have 6 boys left out. How many boys are in the class?

Week 7 Angry Bird

AB-238 A group of fairies went to a small village to give presents to the kids. Some of the fairies had 2 wings and some have 4 wings. There were three times as many fairies with 2 wings as fairies with 4 wings. Altogether, all the fairies had 30 wings. How many fairies went to the village?

Week 8

Week 8 Letter to the Parents

A lot of happy ends...The Number Cruncher was finally able to grab to Angry Bird prize. He jumped around in the library like a kangaroo, catching everyone's eye with his exuberant attitude. But he didn't mind; he was just happy for his achievement. And I was happy I could contribute to his happiness in my humble way.

The Three Little Birds contest finished too. Not with one, but with 3 winners! I gave them all Hexbug Nanos and tracks. It was a big and pleasant surprise for them. They all had a feeling of fulfillment and pride. Way to go!

We went through the last chapter of our mathematical journey – Number Riddles. I saved it for the end because I knew the kids will enjoy it the most and I wasn't wrong.

I told the kids an impressive story about a great Indian mathematician, who made major contributions to several fields in Mathematics despite the hardscrabble existence and a daily struggle to find a stable job.

Week 8 Story – Srinivasa Ramanujan

Srivniavasa Ramanujan was born in Tamil Nadu, India, in 1887. He lived his childhood along with family in the town of Kumbakonam, in a house which is now museum. His father was clerk and his mother was housewife. He also lived with his maternal and paternal grandparents. He was part of the Brahmin cast, so his mother raised him deeply religious and vegetarian. At school, he performed very well, standing first in his district. He read all the books about math that he could get. The book that took Ramanujan's interest in math to a greater level was "A Synopsis of Elementary Results in Pure and Applied Mathematics", which was essentially a collection of 5000 theorems. What is extraordinary about Ramanujan is that he was autodidact; he had very little formal training, and everything he did was without any help. All the great mathematicians in the history had great teachers or mentors who discovered and guided them through their work at the beginning of their career. Isaac Newton wrote in a letter that "If I have seen further it is by standing on the shoulders of giants". But Ramanujan was mostly by himself. He started a correspondence with few English mathematicians. But only one of them, C. H. Hardy, from Cambridge University, became interested in his work. At the beginning, Hardy thought that Ramanujan's work was fraud, since it presented some concepts that were already proven by other mathematicians (Ramanujan couldn't have known that). But there were also concepts that were totally new and Hardy was simply astonished. He had never seen anything like that before. So Hardy, along with colleague, Littlewood, invited Ramanujan to Cambridge. But in accordance with his Brahmin upbringing, Ramanujan refused to leave his country. He accepted however a couple of years later. He spent 5 years in Cambridge, collaborating with Hardy and Littlewood, who were impressed by his work.

The harsh early life and a series of diseases contributed to his very early and regrettable end. He went back to Tamil Nadu in 1919 and died soon thereafter at the age of 32.

Here's a documentary about his life and mathematical talent:

http://www.youtube.com/watch?v=OARGZ1xXCxs

His biography is also impressive: "The Man Who Knew Infinity: A Life of the Genius Ramanujan Paperback" by Robert Kanigel - http://www.amazon.com/The-Man-Who-Knew-Infinity/dp/0671750615/ref=reg_hu-rd_add_1_dp

Week 8 Curriculum – Number Riddles

Level 1

NR1-239 How many numbers from 10 to 99 are there where both digits are even?

NR1-240 What is the largest even number among the following numbers?

87, 11, 22, 99, 45, 48, 68, 73, 44

NR1-241 The houses on my street are numbered with consecutive even numbers. The first house has the number 4 and the last one is numbered 22. How many houses are on my street?

NR1-242 If $9 + X = 24$, how much is $X + X$?

NR1-243 If $12 + 34 = X - 20$, what is X?

NR1-244 $23 + 17 = 20 + X$. Find X.

NR1-245 How many rectangles are in the picture below?

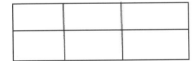

NR1-246 What is the difference between the largest odd number and the smallest even number among the following numbers?

35, 12, 17, 22, 43, 54, 63, 58, 28, 38

NR1-247 The houses on Gene' street are numbered with consecutive odd numbers. Gene's house has the number 5 and there are 6 houses between his house and Sydney's house. What number does Sydney's house have?

NR1-248 What is the largest number among the following, which has an even sum of its digits?

28, 35, 34, 45, 25, 47, 39

Level 2

NR2-249 I am an even number. I am greater than 12, but less than 24. When you count by 5s, you will find me. What number am I?

NR2-250 What is the smallest 2-digit odd number you can make by using 2 of the following numbers?
2, 4, 5, 9, 1, 3

NR2-251 Vlad's dad's age is an odd number. He is older than 27 and younger than Gene's dad. If you count by 5, you will find Vlad's dad's age. If Gene's dad is 38, how old is Vlad's dad?

NR2-252 How many even numbers are there between 13 and 21 that have the sums of their digits also even?

NR2-253 Look at the following numbers: 12, 5, 14, 8, 10. What is the largest difference between 2 of these numbers? What is the smallest?

NR2-254 There are 145 students in the North Hill elementary school. 20 of them are kindergarteners, 25 first graders, 28 second graders, 30 third graders, 22 fourth graders. How many fifth graders are in the school?

NR2-255 There are 6 cards in a box. The cards are numbered 1 through 6. When Gordon takes one card out of the box, the sum of the remaining ones is 16. What card did Gordon take out?

NR2-256 What number must be added to the sum of 15 and 8 to equal the sum of 18 and 17?

NR2-257 Find the sum of all the numbers that are inside the ellipse and outside the square.

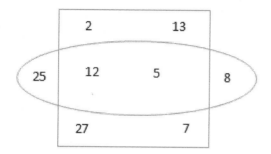

NR2-258 Bobby, Frankie and Josh chose the numbers for their soccer jerseys. The numbers on the jerseys are 7, 12 and 21. Bobby's jersey has an odd number. Frankie's jersey has the largest number. What number is on Josh's jersey?

Level 3

NR3-259 The sum of Vlad's age and Trenton's age is 12. The sum of the Trenton's age and Gene's age is 15. Vlad and Gene were born in the same year. How old is Trenton?

NR3-260 John lives in New York in a sky scraper. One day, he visited Sydney who lives on the 25th floor in the same building. John took the elevator and went up 19 floors, but then he realized that he passed Sydney's floor. He then took the elevator down 8 floors to get to Sydney's floor. On which floor does John live?

NR3-261 A cat, a mouse and a squirrel weigh together 10 pounds. The cat and two mice weigh 8 pounds. The squirrel and 3 mice weigh as much as 2 cats. How much does a squirrel weigh?

NR3-262 A bag of red gems weighs 10 ounces. A bag of red gems together with a bag of white gems weigh as much as 3 bags of red gems. How much do 3 bags of white gems weigh?

NR3-263 I am a number. Add me to myself, then add 12 and subtract 5. You will get 21. What number am I?

NR3-264 Vlad and Gene went to soccer tryouts at the beginning of the season. They sat on the bench along with other kids waiting for their turn. There are 24 kids to the left of Vlad and other 36 kids to the left. Gene sat right in the middle of the bench, with the same number of kids sitting on his left and right side. How many kids were sitting between Gene and Vlad?

NR3-265 Vlad, Daria, and Delilah went to pick apples. Vlad picked 10 apples. Daria picked 12 apples less than Delilah. Delilah picked 3 times more apples than Vlad. How many apples did they all pick?

NR3-266 Vlad, Gene, and Sydney went to Panera Bread to buy snack. Vlad bought 1 muffin, 2 cookies, and 3 bagels, and paid $27. Gene bought 4 muffins, 2 cookies, and 3 bagels, and paid $36. Sydney bought just a muffin and a cookie for $5. How much is a cookie?

NR3-267 Daria and Delilah have $36 together. Daria bought 4 cupcakes with all her money. Delilah paid twice as much for 6 muffins and she spent all her money too. How much does a muffin cost?

NR3-268 X is a number. If I double it, add 12 to it, and then subtract 36, I get again X. What number is X?

Week 8 Three Little Birds

LB-269 Bobby, Frankie and Josh chose the numbers for their soccer jerseys. The numbers on the jerseys are 7, 12 and 21. Bobby's jersey has an odd number. Frankie's jersey has the largest number. What number is on Josh's jersey?

LB-270 The rectangles in the house below cost $5 dollars each and the triangles cost $10 each. How much did the front of the house cost?

LB-271 There are 6 cards in a box. The cards are numbered 1 through 6. When Trenton takes two cards out of the box, the sum of the remaining ones is 11. What cards did Trenton take out?

Week 8 Angry Bird

AB-272 John, Olivia and Ken are the top 3 students in a math tournament. They will all get medals: gold for 1st place, silver for 2nd place, bronze for 3rd place. John and Ken together accumulated 10 points. Ken had 4 more points than John, and Olivia had 2 less points than Ken. What medal is Olivia going to get and with what score?

Math Competitions

I had reviewed a lot of math competitions for 2nd graders before I stopped at 3 of them. Traceable past results, good number of participants, and challenging tests ranked high among my selection criteria.

Noetic Math Contest

The Noetic Learning Math Contest is a biannual problem-solving contest for elementary students in grades 2 – 6. The fall contest is scheduled in November, and the spring contest – in April. To participate in the contest, teachers can organize student teams and register at http://www.noetic-learning.com/mathcontest. Participating teachers will administer the test to the student teams within the contest window. During the contest, students are given 45 minutes to solve 20 problems that can cover a broad range of mathematics skills taught in school. Teachers will grade the test and report the scores. After winners are announced, medals will be sent to the teachers for distribution. One thing about medals – they are very nicely crafted. Heavy, sturdy, shiny, and most importantly, made in US. The kids love them.

Awards:

The top 10% in each grade will receive a 'National Honor Roll' medal and will be announced on their web site. They send an email after they centralize all the results to explain what 10% means in terms of test score. It may be a 90% score or lower, depending on the overall results.

The highest scorer from each team will receive a 'Team Winner' medal.

The top 50% in each grade will only be announced on their web site.

The previous year's tests can be bought from http://www.noetic-learning.com/mathcontest/pasttests.jsp.

Math Kangaroo

Math Kangaroo Competition is an international, once a year event, always on the third Thursday in March.

It is the largest Math competition with more than 6 million kids involved yearly. It is still catching up in the US, with a little bit over 13,000 participants in 2013. The participation by state ranged in 2013 from 8 students in Oklahoma to more than 2,200 in California and Maryland.

Each student receives a t-shirt, a certificate of participation, and a gift in addition to a competition booklet and a pencil on the test day.

The competition comprises a 75 Minutes multiple choice test with 24 questions. No calculators or cell phones are allowed. The questions are categorized in 3 levels of difficulty, and they are scored accordingly: 1/3 of questions are 3 points each, 1/3 - 4 points each, 1/3 - 5 points each. The maximum score is 96.

Awards:

Gold medals are awarded for the first place at each level nationwide. Silver medals are awarded for the second place at each level nationwide. Bronze medals are awarded for the third place at each level nationwide.

Blue Ribbon is awarded for the first place in state. Red Ribbon is awarded for the second place in state. White Ribbon is awarded for the third place in state.

More details: http://www.mathkangaroo.org

Continental Mathematics League

Continental Math League is a competition that started in 1980. It consists in 3 tests taken a month apart in January, February and March. Each test has 6 questions. The scores are cumulative and the awards are distributed after all 3 tests are submitted. Each participating team receives 5 certificates and 2 medals. There is no online registration; an application form has to be downloaded, filled out, and mailed to a PO box in New York, along with check of $75 (for the entire team). The same form can be used to order books.

More information: http://www.continentalmathematicsleague.com/cml.html

Rock and Roll – More Practice Problems

RR-273 One rainy day, Daria, Sydney and Delilah played a card game. There could be only one winner in that game, without any ties. If one player won, the other 2 lost. Daria lost 3 games, Sydney lost 6 games, and Delilah lost 7 games. How many games did Daria win?

RR-274 Vlad picked 36 apples. He gave a half of them to his friend Jacob. Then he gave a third of the remaining ones to his neighbor. But then Jacob said he had too many and he gave 4 apples back to Vlad. Finally, Vlad gave half of the apples to his brother. How many apples was Vlad left with?

RR-275 Sydney, Trenton and Vlad have 64 Christmas cards altogether. Vlad and Sydney have the same number of cards. Trenton and Sydney have together 49 cards. How many cards does Vlad have?

RR-276 Don, John, Terry and Charley are brothers. John is 3 years younger than Terry. Charley is 5 years younger than Terry. Don is 3 years younger than John. Who is the youngest?

RR-277 John is 4 years old. Mark is 7 years older than John and Edward is 5 years younger than Mark. What will be the sum of their ages 5 years later?

RR-278 Vlad has all kinds of coins in his piggy bank – pennies, dimes, nickels, and quarters. What is the minimum number of coins that Vlad would need to pay the exact amount for a notebook that costs 49 cents? What is the maximum number?

RR-279 There are 3 2nd grade classes in North Hill Elementary School. There are 34 students in the first 2 classes combined. There are 8 more students in the first class than in the second, and 3 more in the third than in the second. How many students were in the third 2nd grade class?

RR-280 We are 2-digit numbers. The sum of the 2 digits is 11, and the difference is 5. What numbers are we?

RR-281 Vlad was born in 2005. His mom was 27 years old when he was born. Vlad's sister, Daria, was 4 years old at that time. In what year was his mom born?

RR-282 Gene builds a Lego house with 34 red and yellow pieces of Lego. There are 6 more yellow pieces than red pieces. How many red pieces does Gene have? How many yellow?

RR-283 Daria arranged her collection of marbles in small boxes. She likes patterns, so she put 1 marble in the first box, 2 in the second, 3 in the third and so on. Her collection numbers 36 marbles. How many boxed did she need?

RR-284 Vlad is 5 years older than Daria. The sum of their ages is 19. How old is Daria?

RR-285 Vlad and Daria went to OfficeMax to buy pencils. Vlad bought 2 blue pencils for 13 cents each. Daria saw some red pencils that were sold by the pair – 7 cents each pair. She liked them and bought 8. Who paid more for the pencils? How much more?

RR-286 Vlad has 6 more pencils than Gene. Sydney has as many pencils as Vlad and Gene have together. If Vlad has 13 pencils, how many pencils does Sydney have?

RR-287 Vlad, Sydney, Trenton and Gene wanted to share 3 big cookies so they each had the same amount. Is it possible? If yes, what fraction did each person receive?

RR-288 Vlad bought a total of 12 red and green t-shirts. He bought twice as many green t-shirts as red t-shirts. How many red t-shirts did he buy?

RR-289 22 kids showed up at Vlad's birthday party. He had 3 dozens of cookies and wanted to offer each kid 2 cookies. How many more cookies did he need?

RR-290 John paid for 5 pencils with 4 quarters, 4 dimes, 2 nickels. The following day he needed to buy 10 more pencils for his friend. He only had 3 quarters and 3 dimes. How much more did he need?

RR-291 Trenton and Gene collect postage stamps. Trenton has 21 stamps and gave Gene 6 stamps to have both the same number. How many did Gene have initially?

RR-292 John has 3 pencils, Eric has 3 more pencils than Mark, and Mark has 3 times more pencils than John. How many pencils do they have altogether?

RR-293 The concert had three 40 minutes parts with two equal breaks between the parts. The concert started at 10:20 PM and it finished at 1 AM. How long were the breaks?

RR-294 Vlad bought 4 watermelons and 9 oranges for $36. He paid the same the same amount of money for watermelons as he paid for oranges. He also wanted to buy mangos, but one mango was $2 more expensive than one orange, so he gave up the idea. How much did a mango cost?

RR-295 Trenton paid $21 for 3 notebooks and 3 pencils. Gene paid $11 for 1 notebook and 3 pencils. They also bought 4 erasers. One eraser was $1 cheaper than one pencil. How much did they pay for the erasers?

RR-296 John has a box full of chips with numbers on them. A chip can only have one of the following 3 numbers: 9, 4, 7. John extracts 3 chips and calculates the sum of the numbers written on them. The sum is less than 16 and greater than 12. He then arranges the 3 numbers in ascending order and calculates the sum between the median and the modal. What is the sum that John came up with?

RR-297 Sydney brings 13 marbles, Vlad brings 11 marbles, Trenton brings 8 marbles, and Gene doesn't bring any. They put all the marbles together and divide them equally among themselves. Then Gene takes his share of marbles and gives half of them to his brother, Min. Min plays soccer in a 7-player team. He wants to give one marble to each of his team mates. How many more marbles would he need?

RR-298 Chris was born on June 17th, 2005. Dora was born on Sep 23rd, 2006. John was born on Aug 16th, 2007. Mark was born on Oct 24th, 2007. They decide to get all together on Sep 1st 2013 and have a party. What will be the sum of their ages?

RR-299 The shelter next to Vlad's house has a number of dogs. The difference between their legs and their tails is 27. Every week 2 new dogs are brought to the shelter and 5 dogs are adopted by new families. In how many weeks will the shelter get empty?

RR-300 The distance between city A and city B is 123 miles. The distance between city B and city C is 88 miles. We don't have any information about where these 3 cities are located. What is the minimum distance between A and C? What is the maximum?

Final Note – The Results of the Experiment

12 medals, 2 national honorable mentions, and a 2nd place (red ribbon) in the state of Michigan at Kangaroo Math! All from a 4 student team. But these awards represent only a part the success. The other one, that's closer to my heart, was revealed by the joy I saw in their eyes every time we met, their eagerness to see the Angry Bird or the Three Little Birds, their inquiring gazes, their strong will to solve challenging problems, and their pride of doing something that their classmates have never been exposed to. This is something that 1000 golden medals will never be able to replace. It is the passion for math.

We had a pizza party in our last session and I talked to kids about how they liked our little math club. They all said they liked it and would like to continue the following year. I asked them what they liked the most. Terence Tao and Apollo 13 scored high among their preferences. I felt I accomplished my goal. I wanted the kids to enjoy doing math and not consider it like just another tiresome drudgery. I wanted the kids to discover new role models to look up to, to dream about.

Now I look forward to the next year. There will be new challenges, new competitions, effort and commitment, but at least I know for sure that I have a good team, with students willing to work hard and aspire high.

Solutions

Week 1

Level 1

ML1-003 Jack bought a pirates puzzle that had 20 pieces less than the cars puzzle which he already had. The pirates puzzle had 50 pieces. How many pieces did the cars puzzle have?

Identify the subjects
Pirate puzzle pieces (P) and Car puzzle pieces (C)
Sketch the facts. What do we know about the subjects?

Fact 1:   The   pirate   puzzle   has   50   pieces
Fact 2: The pirate puzzle has 20 pieces less than the car puzzle

So we'll have to take away 20 pieces from the pirate puzzle to find out how many pieces are in the car puzzle.

Write the solution
(C) : 50 − 20 = 30 pieces

The car puzzle has 30 pieces.

ML1-004 Justin and his sister, Helen went shopping. Justin bought 60 markers. If he bought 20 fewer markers than his sister, how many did Helen buy?

Identify the subjects
Justin (J) and Helen (H)

Sketch the facts. What do we know about the subjects?

Fact 1:   Justin   bought   60   markers
Fact 2: Justin bought 20 fewer markers than Helen

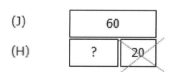

So we'll have to take away 20 markers from Justin to find out how many markers Helen bought.
Write the solution
(H) : 60 − 20 = 40 markers

Helen bought 40 markers.

ML1-005 Gene bought a donut that was 15 cents less expensive than a muffin. The price of the donut was 25 cents. How much did the muffin cost?

Identify the subjects
Donut (D) and Muffin (M)

Sketch the facts. What do we know about the subjects?

Fact 1: The donut costs 50 cents
Fact 2: The donut is 15 cents less expensive than the muffin

(D) | 50 |
(M) | 50 | 15 |

Write the solution
(M) : 50 + 15 = 65 cents

The muffin costs 65 cents.

ML1-006 For the art class, the teacher brought some red and blue ribbons. There are 5 fewer blue ribbons than red ribbons. If there are 12 blue ribbons, how many red ribbons are there?

Identify the subjects
Red ribbons (J) and Blue ribbons (B)

Sketch the facts. What do we know about the subjects?

Fact 1: There are 12 blue ribbons
Fact 2: There are 5 fewer blue ribbons than red

(B) | 12 |
(R) | 12 | 5 |

So we'll have to add 5 to the number of blue ribbons to find the number of red ribbons.
Write the solution
(R) : 12 + 5 = 17 ribbons

The teacher brought 17 ribbons.

ML1-007 At the grocery store, an apple costs 50 cents. The price of the apple is 25 cents higher than the price of the banana. How much does the banana costs?

Identify the subjects

Apple (A) and Banana (B)

Sketch the facts. What do we know about the subjects?

Fact 1: An apple costs 50 cents
Fact 2: The apple costs 25 cents more than the banana

Write the solution
(B) : 50 +2 5 = 75 cents

The banana costs 74 cents

ML1-008 Trenton's desk is 90 centimeters tall. The desk is 30 centimeters taller than his chair. How tall is his chair?

Identify the subjects
Desk (D) and Chair (C)

Sketch the facts. What do we know about the subjects?

Fact 1: The desk is 90 cm tall
Fact 2: The desk is 30 cm taller than the chair

(D) | 90 |
(C) | ? | 30 |

Write the solution
(C) : 90 - 30 = 60 cm

The chair is 60 cm tall.

ML1-009 Vlad picked 15 apples and some peaches from the orchard. He picked 7 more peaches than apples. How many peaches did he harvest?

Identify the subjects
Apples (A) and Peaches (P)

Sketch the facts. What do we know about the subjects?

Fact 1: Vlad picked 15 apples
Fact 2: Vlad picked 7 more peaches than apples

(A) | 15 |
(P) | 15 | 7 |

Write the solution
(P) : 15 + 7 = 22 peaches

Vlad picked 22 peaches.

ML1-010 Mother is 26 years younger than Grandpa and she is now 30 year old. How old is Grandpa?

Identify the subjects
Mother (M) and Grandpa (G)

Sketch the facts. What do we know about the subjects?

Fact 1: Mother is 30 year old
Fact 2: Mother is 26 years younger than Grandpa

(M) | 30 |
(G) | 30 | 26 |

Write the solution
(G) : 30 + 26 = 56 years

Grandpa is 56 years old.

Level 2

ML2-012. Gene scored 8 goals during the soccer game last Saturday. Vlad scored 3 goals. How many fewer goals did Vlad score?

Identify the subjects

Gene (G) and Vlad (V)

Sketch the facts. What do we know about the subjects?

Fact 1: Gene scored 8 goals

Fact 2: Vlad scored 3 goals

(G) [8]

(V) [3][?]

3 + ? = 8

Write the solution

8 − 3 = 5

Vlad scored 5 goals fewer than Gene.

ML2-013. Dwayne is 55 inches tall. His younger brother, Dustin, is 40 inches tall. How much shorter is Dustin?

Identify the subjects

Dwayne (Dw) and Dustin (Du)

Sketch the facts. What do we know about the subjects?

Fact 1: Dwayne is 55 inches tall

Fact 2: Dustin is 40 inches tall

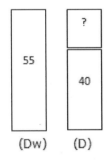

40 + ? = 55   55 − 40 = 15

Write the solution

Dustin is 15 inches shorter than Dwayne.

ML2-014. An helicopter can fly up to 1,000 feet above the ground. A commercial airplane can go to 6,000 feet above the ground. How much higher can the airplane fly?

Identify the subjects

Helicopter (H) and airplane (A)

Sketch the facts. What do we know about the subjects?

Fact 1: The helicopter can fly 1,000 feet above the ground

Fact 2: The airplane can fly 1,000 feet above the ground

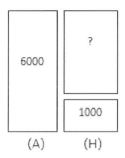

1000 + ? = 6000; 6000 − 1000 = 5000

Write the solution

A commercial airplane can fly 5000 feet higher than the helicopter.

ML2-015. Adam is 8 years old. His grandpa is 78. How much older is his grandpa?

Identify the subjects

Adam (A) and Grandpa (G)

Sketch the facts. What do we know about the subjects?

Fact 1: Adam is 8 years old

Fact 2: Grandpa is 78 years old

(G) | 78 |
(A) | 8 | ? |

8 + ? = 78;   78 − 8 = 70

Write the solution

Grandpa is 70 years older than Adam.

ML2-016. In the professional soccer leagues, the goals are 8 yards wide. In the youth leagues, they can be 3 yards wide. How much wider are the goals used in the professional soccer leagues?

Identify the subjects

Professional league goals (P) and youth league goals (Y)

Sketch the facts. What do we know about the subjects?

Fact 1: The goals in professional leagues are 8 yards long

Fact 2: The goals in youth leagues are 3 yards long

(G) | 8 |
(A) | 3 | ? |

3 + ? = 8; 8 − 3 = 5

Write the solution

The goals in professional league soccer are 5 yards wider than in youth league.

ML2-017. A sack of beans weighs 20 pounds. A bag of lentils weighs 28 pounds. How much heavier are the lentils?

28 − 20 = 8

The bag of lentils is 8 pounds heavier that the sack of beans.

ML2-018. Trenton and Sydney are getting ready for the Math Pentathlon tournament. They play a Hex-A-Gone game together. Trenton has placed 7 pieces on the board and 2 of them were hexagons. Sydney placed 10 pieces and 4 of them were diamonds. How many more pieces did Sydney place on the board?

The problem only asks about the number of pieces, not about their shapes. The fact that 2 out of Trenton's 7 pieces are hexagons and 4 out of Sydney's 10 pieces are diamonds is not relevant, and can be skipped.

Identify the subjects

Trenton (T) and Sydney (S)

Sketch the facts. What do we know about the subjects?

Fact 1: Trenton placed 7 pieces.

Fact 2: Sydney placed 10 pieces

(S) | 10 |

(T) | 7 | ? |

$7 + ? = 10; \quad 10 - 7 = 3$

Write the solution

Sydney placed 3 more pieces on the board.

ML2-019. Maia and John counted the money in their piggy banks. Maia has $5.37 and John has $10.15. How much more money does John have?

Identify the subjects

Maia (M) and John (J)

Sketch the facts. What do we know about the subjects?

Fact 1: Maia has $5.37.

Fact 2: John has $10.15

$10.15 - 5.37 = 4.78$

Write the solution

John has $4.78 more than Maia.

ML2-020. Daria solved 297 math problems over the summer. Vlad solved 119. How many less problems did Vlad solve than Daria?

Identify the subjects

Daria (D) and Vlad (V)

Sketch the facts. What do we know about the subjects?

Fact 1: Daria solved 297 problems.

Fact 2: Vlad solved 119 problems.

$297 - 119 = 78$

Write the solution

Vlad solved 78 less problems than Daria.

Level 3

ML3-022 Mr. Vlassopoulos uses 20 balls in his sports class. There are 8 more soccer balls than tennis balls. How many soccer balls is he using?

Identify the subjects

Soccer balls (S) and Tennis balls (T)

Sketch the facts. What do we know about the subjects?

Fact 1: There are 8 more soccer balls than tennis balls.

(T) ▯

(S) ▯ 8

Fact2: There are 20 balls altogether:

(T) + (S) = ▯ ▯ 8
            └──── 20 ────┘

Subtract 8 to get the sum of the 2 equal rectangles:

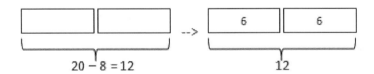

20 − 8 = 12   12

Write the solution

Let's now back to the Fact 1 and write the result:

(T) [6]   = 6

(S) [6][8]   = 14

There are 14 soccer balls.

Check the results:
Fact 1: Are there 8 more soccer balls than tennis balls? Yes (14 = 6 + 8)
Fact 2: Are there 20 balls altogether? Yes (6 + 14 = 20)

ML3-023 Hana and Diane arranged their jumping ropes head to head and measured them. The two ropes together measured 110 inches. Hana's rope is 30 inches shorter than Diane's. How long is Diane's rope?

Identify the subjects

Hana's rope (H) and Diane's rope (D)

Sketch the facts. What do we know about the subjects?

Fact 1: Hana's rope is 30 inches shorter than Diane's.

(H) ☐
(D) ☐ 30

Fact2: The two ropes together measured 110 inches:

(H) + (D) = ☐ ☐ 30
              └─── 110 ───┘

Subtract 30 to get the sum of the 2 equal rectangles:

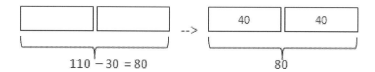

110 − 30 = 80   80

Write the solution

Let's now go back to the Fact 1 and write the result:

(H) [40]   = 40
(D) [40][30]   = 70

Diane's rope is 70 inches long.

Check the results:
Fact 1: Is Hana's rope 30 inches shorter? Yes (70 = 40 + 30)
Fact 2: Do the 2 ropes measure 110 together? Yes (70 + 40 = 110)

ML3-024. Gene and Sydney put their money together to buy a board game. They had 17 dollars together. Gene had 3 dollars more than Sydney. How much money did Sydney have?

Identify the subjects

Gene's money (G) and Sydney's money (S)

Sketch the facts. What do we know about the subjects?

Fact 1: Gene had 3 dollars more than Sydney.

(S) [   ]
(G) [   ] [3]

Fact 2: They had 17 dollars together:

(S) + (G) = [   ][   ][3]
            _____/
                   17

Subtract 3 to get the sum of the 2 equal rectangles:

[   ][   ] --> [7][7]
_____/   ____/
 17 − 3 = 14   14

Write the solution

Let's now go back to the Fact 1 and write the result:

(S) [7]   = 7
(G) [7] [3]   = 10

Sydney had 7 dollars.

Check the results:
Fact 1: Did Gene have 3 dollars more than Sydney? Yes (10 = 7 + 3)
Fact 2: Do they have 17 dollars together? Yes (10 + 7 = 17)

ML3-025. The ages of Jack's mom and dad add up to 64 years. His dad is 4 years older than his mom. How old is his mom?

Identify the subjects

Mom's age (M) and Dad's age (D)

Sketch the facts. What do we know about the subjects?

Fact 1: Dad is 4 years older than mom.

(M) ▭

(D) ▭ 4

Fact2: Mom and dad's ages add up to 64 years:

(M) + (D) = ▭ ▭ 4 }_{64}

Subtract 4 to get the sum of the 2 equal rectangles:

Write the solution

Let's now go back to the Fact 1 and write the result:

(M) [30]   = 30

(D) [30] [4]   = 34

Jack's mom is 30 years old.

Check the results:
Fact 1: Dad is 4 years older than mom: 34 = 30 + 4
Fact2: Mom and dad's ages add up to 64 years: 30 + 34 = 64

ML3-026. There are 123 white and black marbles in a jar. The number of white marbles is 47 greater than the number of black marbles. How many white marbles are in the jar?

Identify the subjects

White marbles (W) and Black marbles (B)

Sketch the facts. What do we know about the subjects?

Fact 1: The number of white marbles is 47 greater than the number of black marbles.

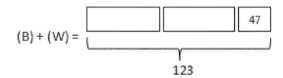

Fact2: There are 123 white and black marbles in the jar:

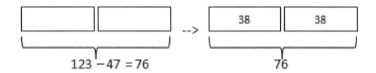

Subtract 47 to get the sum of the 2 equal rectangles:

Write the solution

Let's now go back to the Fact 1 and write the result:

(B) [38]   = 38
(W) [38][47]   = 85

There are 85 marbles in the jar.

Check the results:
Fact 1: The number of white marbles is 47 greater than the number of black marbles: 85 = 38 + 47
Fact2: There are 123 white and black marbles in the jar: 38 + 85 = 123

ML3-027. Uncle John has apple trees and cherry trees in his orchard, 46 in all. There are 12 more apple trees than cherry trees. How many cherry trees does Uncle John have?

Identify the subjects

Apple trees (A) and Cherry trees (C)

Sketch the facts. What do we know about the subjects?

Fact 1: There are 12 more apple trees than cherry trees.

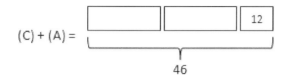

Fact2: There are 46 trees in the orchard:

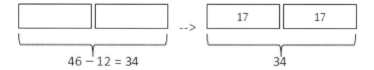

Subtract 12 to get the sum of the 2 equal rectangles:

[diagram: two equal rectangles with 46 − 12 = 34 → two rectangles labeled 17 and 17 with sum 34]

Write the solution

Let's now go back to the Fact 1 and write the result:

(C) [17] = 17
(A) [17][12] = 29

Uncle John has 17 cherry trees.

Check the results:
Fact 1: There are 12 more apple trees than cherry trees: 29 = 17 + 12
Fact2: There are 46 trees in the orchard: 17 + 29 = 36

ML3-028. The students in Mrs. Mustola class have to arrange the tables and the chairs in the school's festivity hall. They counted 76 tables and chairs together. There are 38 more chairs than tables. How many tables are there in the festivity hall?

Identify the subjects

Tables (T) and Chairs (C)

Sketch the facts. What do we know about the subjects?

Fact 1: There are 38 more chairs than tables.

(T) ▭
(C) ▭ 38

Fact2: There are 76 tables and chairs together:

(T) + (C) =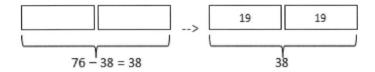
76

Subtract 38 to get the sum of the 2 equal rectangles:

▭ ▭ --> 19 19
76 − 38 = 38   38

Write the solution

Let's now go back to the Fact 1 and write the result:

(T) 19   = 19
(C) 19 38   = 57

There are 19 tables in the hall.

Check the results:
Fact 1: There are 38 more chairs than tables: 57 = 19 + 38
Fact2: There are 76 tables and chairs together: 19 + 57 = 76

ML3-029. Daria went to the farmers market and bought apples and peaches. She counted them all and got 87 fruits. She bought 29 more apples than peaches. How many apples did she buy?

Identify the subjects

Apples (A) and Peaches (C)

Sketch the facts. What do we know about the subjects?

Fact 1: Daria bought 29 more apples than peaches.

(P) ▭
(A) ▭ 29

Fact2: Daria bought 87 fruits:

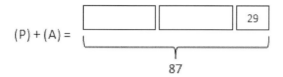

Subtract 29 to get the sum of the 2 equal rectangles:

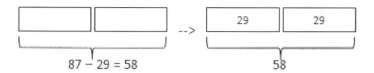

Write the solution

Let's now go back to the Fact 1 and write the result:

(P) [29]   = 29
(A) [29][29] = 58

Daria bought 58 apples.

Check the results:
Fact 1: Daria bought 29 more apples than peaches: 58 = 29 + 29
Fact2: Daria bought 87 fruits: 58 + 29 = 87

ML3-030. Vlad's grandpa raises sheep and cows in his farm. There are 45 animals altogether and there are 19 more sheep than cows. How many sheep does the grandpa have?

Identify the subjects

Sheep (S) and Cows (C)

Sketch the facts. What do we know about the subjects?

Fact 1: There are 19 more sheep than cows.

(C) [   ]
(S) [   ][19]

Fact2: There are 45 animals altogether:

Subtract 19 to get the sum of the 2 equal rectangles:

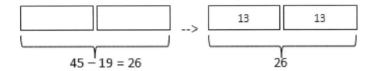

Write the solution

Let's now go back to the Fact 1 and write the result:

(C) [13]   = 13
(S) [13][19]   = 32

Grandpa has 32 sheep.

Check the results:
Fact 1: There are 19 more sheep than cows: 32 = 13 + 19
Fact2: There are 45 animals altogether: 13 + 32 = 45

Three Little Birds

LB-031 Vlad has 6 more pencils than Gene. Sydney has as many pencils as Vlad and Gene have together. If Vlad has 13 pencils, how many pencils does Sydney have?

Identify the subjects

Vlad (V), Gene (G) and Sydney (S)

Sketch the facts. What do we know about the subjects?

Fact 1: Vlad has 6 more pencils than Gene.

(G) [   ]
(V) [   ][6]

Fact2: Sydney has as many pencils as Vlad and Gene have together:

(S) [   ][6]

Fact 3: Vlad has 13 pencils:

(V) [___ | 6] = 13 → [___] = 13 − 6 = 7

Write the solution

Let's now go back to the Fact 2 and write the result:

(S) [7 | 7 | 6] = 20

Sydney has 20 pencils.

Check the results:
Fact 1: Vlad has 6 more pencils than Gene. Vlad has 7 + 6 = 13 pencils and Gene has 7 pencils.
Fact2: Sydney has as many pencils as Vlad and Gene have together (13 + 7 = 20)

LB-032 Vlad and Daria worked on their homework together yesterday. Vlad had to complete 27 math problems and Daria 36 problems. They took a break right after Vlad finished 10 problems and Daria finished 12 problems. How many less problems did Vlad completed after the break than Daria did after the break?

Fact 1: The total number of problems is 27 for Vlad and 36 for Daria.

Fact 2: Before the break, Vlad finished 10 problems and Daria finished 12 problems.

	Vlad	Daria
Before break	10	12
After break	?	?
Total	27	36

27 − 10 = 17
36 − 12 = 24

So Vlad did 17 problems after the break and Daria did 24.

	Vlad	Daria
Before break	10	12
After break	17	24
Total	27	36

24 − 17 = 7

So Vlad completed 7 less problems than Daria.

LB-033 Vlad has 23 balloons and Sydney has 32. If Sydney will give Vlad 8 balloons, she will have _____ less balloons than Vlad.

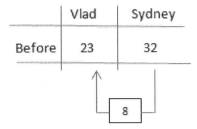

Sydney gives Vlad 8 balloons, so Vlad has 8 more and Sydney has 8 less:

	Vlad	Sydney
After	23+8=31	32-8=24

How many less balloons does Sydney have now?

31 – 24 = 7

Answer: Sydney has 7 less balloons than Vlad.

Angry Bird

AB-034 Vivian, Alex and Sophie have 140 balloons altogether. Vivian and Alex have the same number of balloons. Alex and Sophie have together 82 balloons. How many balloons does Alex have?

Fact 1. Vivian and Alex have the same number of balloons
Because Vivian and Alex have the same number of balloons, we'll use the same symbol for them:

Vivian   Alex   Sophie
  ○   ○   □

Fact 2. Alex and Sophie have together 82 balloons
Fact 3. Vivian, Alex and Sophie have 140 balloons altogether

Let's sketch these 2 facts now:

○ + ○ + □ = 140

○ + □ = 82

We can visually notice that the 2 number sentences (I don't call them equations yet) are similar. It is just a circle that they differ by. So we can find the value of the circle by subtracting the 2 numbers:

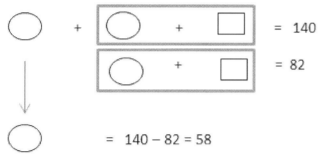

We now have to find the value of the square. We use Fact 2 for that.

 + ☐ = 82

So the value of the square is:

☐ = 82 − 58 = 24

We have now the number of balloons for every kid:

Vivian   Alex   Sophie

(58)   (58)   [24]

The problem asked for the number of balloons that Alex had, so we didn't even have to find the value of the square. But we did it anyway, to have a full picture of the problem.

Week 2

Level 1

DT01-037. Jack's brother is exactly 3 years old. How many months old is he?
1 year = 12 months
2 years = 24 months
3 years = 36 months

DT01-038. The soccer season lasted 5 weeks. How many days long was the season?

Solution:
1 week = 7 days
2 weeks = 14 days
3 weeks = 21 days
4 weeks = 28 days
5 weeks = 35 days

DT01-039. It takes 40 hours for Dylan's sailboat to get from Port Huron to Mackinac Island. The Fudge Festival will start in exactly 2 days. Will Dylan have enough time to get there?

Solution:

1 day = 24 hours
2 days = 48 hours
Dylan will be late for the stat of the festival.

DT01-040. The first pilgrims moved to America in 1620. Christopher Columbus arrived there in 1492. Who got there first?

1492 < 1620, so Columbus was there first.

DT01-041. John went in a 3 month vacation to Hawaii. He said he stayed there 9 weeks. Was he right?

1 month = 4 weeks
2 months = 8 weeks
3 months = 12 weeks

John wasn't right. He stayed in Hawaii 12 weeks.

DT01-042. Which of the following statements are true?

A. One year has 300 days. False: 1 year has 365 days
B. 2 years have 24 months. True
C. 2 years have 100 weeks. False: 1 year has 54 weeks, 2 years have 108 weeks

DT01-043. Because of the storm, Sonia had to stay in the airport 50 hours. Was that more or less than 2 days?

1 day = 24 hours
2 days = 48 hours

Sonia spent less than 50 hours in the airport.

DT01-044. Brian spent 2 months last summer at his grandparents' house in Michigan's Upper Peninsula. He was there in July and August. How many days did he spend there?

July has 31 days
August has 31 days
Brian spend 62 days at his grandparents' house.

Level 2

DT02-048. Joe's birthday is 3 days after Maya's. This year, Maya's birthday is the third Wednesday in October. What is the date of Joe's birthday?

October						
Su	Mo	Tu	We	Th	Fr	Sa
		1	2	3	4	5
6	7	8	9	10	11	12
13	14	15	16	17	18	19
20	21	22	23	24	25	26
27	28	29	30	31		

The third Wednesday in October is the 16th. 3 days after that is the 19th. Joe's birthday is Oct 19th.

DT02-049. In 7 minutes, it will be 7:00 PM. What time is it now?

6:53 PM

DT02-050. A tornado watch was in effect for the Oakland County from 9:30 PM last night to 3:30 AM this morning. How long did the tornado watch last?

Quickly draw a watch:

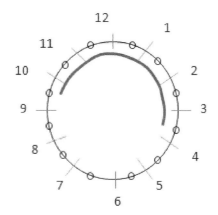

9:30 – 10:30 1 hour
9:30 – 11:30 2 hours
9:30 – 12:30 3 hours
9:30 – 1:30 4 hours
9:30 – 2:30 5 hours
9:30 – 3:30 6 hours
The tornado watch lasted 6 hours.

DT02-051. Our neighbors left home for a cruise on Thursday. They returned home 11 days later. What day of the week did they return home?

Quickly write the days of the week, or use the month picture from DT02-048.
Or, even better, try to do it mentally. A week has 7 days, so 7 days from Wednesday will be a Wednesday. 8 – Thursday, 9 – Friday, 10 – Saturday, 11 – Sunday. The neighbors returned on Sunday.

DT02-052. Today is October 10, 2012. Vlad is 7 years old. How old will he be on October 10, 2020?

There are 8 years between 2012 and 2020. So Vlad is going to be 15 in 2020 (7 + 8 = 15)

DT02-053. The Math workshop starts at 6:00 PM. Today Gene was 12 minutes late to the workshop. What time did Gene come?

12 minutes after 6 PM - 6:12PM

DT02-054. Today is Wednesday. Sydney's birthday was 4 days ago. On what day of the week was Sydney's birthday?

Go backwards 4 days: 1 day – Thursday, 2 days – Monday, 3 days – Sunday, 4 days – Saturday
Sydney's birthday was on Saturday.

Level 3

DT03-057. Vlad leaves school at 4 o'clock. He has lunch at school 5 hours before he leaves. What time does he have lunch?

4 o'clock is 4 hours from noon. So Vlad had lunch 1 hour before noon – that's 11 AM

DT03-058. A part of Mrs. Mustola's Friday class schedule didn't come up from the printer. If we know that each class is 45 minutes long, and there is no break between classes, what time does Physical Education class start?

9:00 - Math Centers
??? - Writing
??? - Art
??? - Physical Education

Solution:

Each class is 45 minutes long:
9:00 - Math Centers
9:45 - Writing
10:30 - Art
11:15 - Physical Education

Answer: Physical Education class starts at 11:15 AM

DT03-059. There are 5 trains every day that travel between Detroit and Grand Rapids. The departure times are as follows:

6:00 AM, 8:12 AM, 9:44 AM, 10:45 AM, 3:56 PM

The trip takes 3 hours and 15 minutes. If it is 10 AM now, what will be the earliest time I can get to Grand Rapids?

It is 10 AM now, so the next trail will depart at 10:45 AM. I add 3 hours and 15 minutes to that, and I find that the earliest time I can get to Grand Rapids is 2 PM.

DT03-060. Trenton takes the bus to school at 8 AM and he returns home with the same bus at 4 PM. He spends 45 minutes in the bus going to school, and 30 minutes coming back from school. He also has 1 hour recess. The rest of the time he stays only in the class. How much time does he spend in the class?

Trenton stays at school from 8 AM to 4 PM, that is 8 hours.

He spends 45 + 30 = 75 minutes in the bus. That's 1 hour and 15 minutes

He has 1 hour recess. So he spends in class 8 hours – 1 hour and 15 minutes – 1 hour = 5 hours and 45 minutes.

DT03-061. The indoor playground at KidsPlay is open Monday through Friday from 10 AM to 9 PM. It is also open on Saturday from 10 AM to 5 PM. It is closed on Sunday. How many hours a week is the playground open?

The playground is open Monday-Friday from 10 AM to 9 PM – that is 11 hours daily, 5 days a week (11 + 11 + 11 + 11 + 11 = 55 hours)
On Saturday, the playground is open from 10 AM to 5 PM – that is 7 hours

So the playground is open 55 + 7 = 62 hours a week

DT03-062. These are the first 3 finishers in the Brooksie Half Marathon:
Alexander West - 1 hour 15 minutes 9 seconds
Shane Logan - 1 hour 13 minutes 15 seconds
Ryan Beck - 1 hour 14 minutes 51 seconds
Who got the gold medal?

Answer: Shane Logan had the best time.

DT03-063. Today is 10/10/2012. No item can be sold after the "Sell by" date. Which of the following items can't be sold today?
Cheese - Sell by 12/10/2012
Milk - Sell by 10/12/2012
Butter - Sell by 9/10/2012

Answer: Butter – it expired yesterday.

DT03-064. When I was 2 my brother had half my age. Now I am 100 years old. How old is my brother?

Solution: When I was 2, my brother was 1, so he is 1 year younger than me. Now I am 100, so my brother is 99 years old.

Three Little Birds

LB-065 Last night it snowed all through the night from 9 PM until 6 AM. For the first 4 hours, 3 inches of snow fell every hour. Then it slowed down, and only 2 inches of snow fell every hour. What was the accumulation of snow at 6 AM in the morning?

9 PM --- 10 PM --- 11 PM --- 12 AM --- 1 AM --- 2 AM ---3 AM --- 4 AM --- 5 AM --- 6 AM

   3"   3"   3"   3"   2"   2"   2"   2"   2"

It snowed continuously for 9 hours.
The accumulation in the first 4 hours was 3 + 3 + 3 + 3 = 12 inches
The accumulation in the last 5 hours was 2 + 2 +2 + 2 + 2 = 10 inches
The total accumulation was 12 + 10 = 22 inches
Answer: 22 inches

LB-066 There are twice as many red pencils as blue pencils in a box. If 5 red pencils are removed from the box, the number of red pencils will be the same as the number of blue pencils. How many blue pencils are in the box?

Fact 1. There are twice as many red pencils as blue pencils:

Blue Pencils   Red Pencils (twice as many)

Fact 2. If 5 red pencils are removed from the box, the number of red pencils will be the same as the number of blue pencils

If we remove a square from the Red pencils side, the number will become the same:

Blue Pencils   Red Pencils (twice as many)

□   □ ⌐ ─ ┐
                       └ ─ ┘
                       └ ─ ─ ─ ─ ─ ─ ─ → Remove 5 pencils

So every square represents 5 pencils:

Blue Pencils   Red Pencils (twice as many)

[5]   [5] [5]

Answer: There are 5 blue pencils in the box

LB-067 Sydney bought a tea kettle and a set of tea cups for $110. If the kettle costs $80 more than the set of cups, how much does the kettle cost?

Fact 1. The kettle costs $80 more than the set of cups

Kettle: □ [80   ]
Cups: □

Fact 2. The tea kettle and the set of tea cups cost together $110

□ + [80   ] + □ = 110

Find the sum of the 2 small rectangles

□ + □ = 110 − 80 = 30

So one rectangle will be half of 30, that's 15. Back to Fact 1:

Kettle: [15] [80   ] = 95
Cups: [15]   = 15

The kettle costs $95.

Angry Bird

AB-068 If Greg gave Tom 4 dimes, he would still have 8 more dimes than Tom. If Tom started with 10 dimes, how many dimes did Greg start with?

Greg has more dimes than Tom. Tom started with 10 dimes:

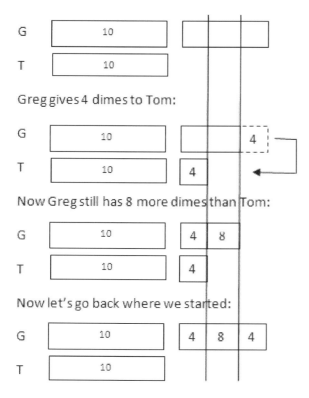

Greg gives 4 dimes to Tom:

Now Greg still has 8 more dimes than Tom:

Now let's go back where we started:

Tom had initially 10 dimes.

Greg started with 10 + 4 + 8 + 4 = 26 dimes

Week 3

Level 1

PT01-072. Continue the sequence:
45, 56, 67, ___, ___
Ascending order. Rule: +11
45, 56, 67, 78, 89

PT01-073. Continue the sequence:
89, 81, 73, ___, ___
Descending order. Rule: -8
89, 81, 73, 65, 57

PT01-074. Continue the sequence:
88, 88, 79, 79, 70, ___, ___
Descending order. Rule: Subtract 9 from every second number.

88, 88, 79, 79, 70, 70, 61

PT01-075. Continue the sequence:
34, 45, 56, ___, ___

Ascending order. Rule: +11

34, 45, 56, 67, 78

PT01-076. Continue the sequence:
121, 102, 83, ___, ___

Descending order. Rule: -19

121, 102, 83, 64, 45

PT01-077. Continue the sequence:

4, 4, 22, 22, 40, ___, ___

Ascending order. Rule: Add 18 to every second number.

4, 4, 22, 22, 40, 58, 76

PT01-078. Continue the sequence:
84, 69, 44, ___, ___

Descending order. Rule: -15

84, 69, 44, 29, 14

Level 2

PT02-082. Continue the sequence:
18, 18, 16, 14, 14, 12, 10, 10, 8, ___, ___

Rule: Subtract 2 from every second and third number.

18, 18, 16, 14, 14, 12, 10, 10, 8, 6, 6

PT02-083. Continue the sequence:
6, 18, 12, 24, 18, 30, 24, 36, 30, ___, ___

Rule: Add 12 and then subtract 6

6, 18, 12, 24, 18, 30, 24, 36, 30, 42, 36

PT02-084. Continue the sequence:
24, 23, 20, 19, 16, 15, 12, 11, 8, ___, ___

Rule: Subtract 1 and then subtract 3

24, 23, 20, 19, 16, 15, 12, 11, 8, 7, 4

PT02-085. Continue the sequence:
24, 29, 27, 32, 30, ___, ___

Rule: Add 5 and then subtract 2

24, 29, 27, 32, 30, 35, 33

PT02-086. Continue the sequence:
121, 131, 135, 145, 149, ___, ___

Rule: Add 10 and then add 4

121, 131, 135, 145, 149, 159, 163

PT02-087. Continue the sequence:
17, 22, 29, 34, 41, ___, ___

Rule: Add 5 and then add 7

17, 22, 29, 34, 41, 46, 53

PT02-088. Continue the sequence:
94, 99, 89, 94, 104, ___, ___

Rule: Add 6 and then subtract 10

94, 99, 89, 94, 84, 89, 79

Level 3

PT03-092. Continue the sequence:
8, 10, 18, 28, 46, ___, ___

Rule: Sum of the previous 2 numbers

8, 10, 18, 28, 46, 74, 120

PT03-093. Continue the sequence:
12, 10, 8, 14, 4, 18, 0, ___

Rule: Add the first 2 numbers and subtract the third.

12, 10, 8, 14, 4, 18, 0, 22

PT03-094. Continue the sequence:
2, 4, 6, 12, 22, 40, ___, ___

Rule: Add the previous 3 numbers

2, 4, 6, 12, 22, 40, 74, 136

PT03-095. Continue the sequence:
2, 4, 6, 10, 16, ___, ___

Rule: Sum of the previous 2 numbers

2, 4, 6, 10, 16, 26, 42

PT03-096. Continue the sequence:
12, 13, 14, 39, 66, ___, ___

Rule: Sum of the previous 3 numbers

12, 13, 14, 39, 66, 119, 224

PT03-097. Continue the sequence:

3, 9, 5, 7, 7, 5, 9, 3, ___, ___

Rule: Add first 2 numbers and subtract the third

3, 9, 5, 7, 7, 5, 9, 3, 11, 1

PT03-098. Continue the sequence:

2, 3, 4, 9, 16, 29, ___, ___

Rule: Sum of the previous 3 numbers

2, 3, 4, 9, 16, 29, 54, 99

Three Little Birds

LB-099. Joe is 3'10" tall. His younger brother, Moe, is 2'4" tall. Their father, Dustin, is as tall as Joe and Moe together. How much taller is Dustin than Joe?

1' = 12"

3'10" + 2'4" = 5'14" We can go on and say 5'14" is actually 6'2" but this is not what the problem asks.

We have to determine how much taller is 5'14" than 3'10". Subtract feet from feet and inches from inches and we get:

5'14" –
3'10"
------   Answer: 2' 4"
2' 4"

The Engineer had a very nice solution for this problem, much better than the one above I would say. He converted all the heights to inches and then he did the calculations:

Joe is 46" tall
Moe is 28" tall
Dustin is 46" + 28" = 74"
So Dustin is 74"-46" = 28" taller than Joe

LB-100. Jack has 2 math worksheets due tomorrow. There are 13 problems in one worksheet and he completed 5 of them. There are 15 problems in the other worksheet and he completed 8 of them. How many math problems does Jack have left to do altogether?

Problems left in worksheet 1: 13 – 5 = 8

Problems left in worksheet 2: 15 – 8 = 7

Total problems left to do: 8 + 7 = 15

LB-101. Two 2nd grade classes went on a field trip to Dinosaur Hill. Each class had 11 students, 1 teacher, 1 para-professional, and 1 parent. How many people went on a field trip?

1 class had 11 + 1 + 1 + 1 = 14 people

2 classes have 14 + 14 = 28 people

Answer: 28 people

Angry Bird

AB-102. Nick had an equal number of pennies, nickels and dimes. Robert has twice as many nickels as Nick. He also has 4 more pennies and 3 more dimes than Nick has. Robert has 9 pennies. How much money does Robert have in total?

There are quite a few facts to sketch here:
Fact 1. Nick had an equal number of pennies, nickels and dimes.
Fact 2. Robert has twice as many nickels as Nick.
Fact 3. Robert also has 4 more pennies than Nick
Fact 4. Robert has 3 more dimes than Nick
Fact 5. Robert has 9 pennies

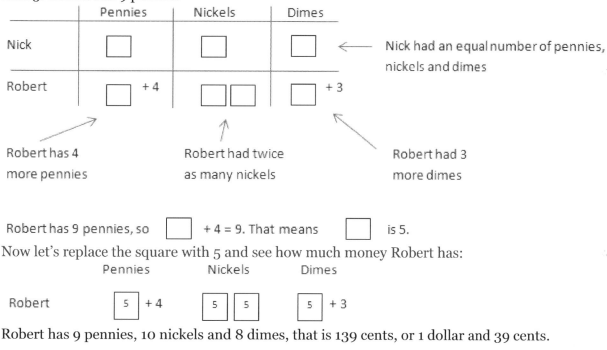

Robert has 9 pennies, 10 nickels and 8 dimes, that is 139 cents, or 1 dollar and 39 cents.

Week 4

Level 1

FR1-105 Arrange the fractions in order, beginning with the smallest:

$$\frac{1}{8} \qquad \frac{1}{2} \qquad \frac{1}{9} \qquad \frac{1}{4} \qquad \frac{1}{12}$$

The **numerators** are all the same, so the smallest fraction is the one with the greatest denominator:

$$\frac{1}{12} \qquad \frac{1}{9} \qquad \frac{1}{8} \qquad \frac{1}{4} \qquad \frac{1}{2}$$

FR1-106 Compare the following fractions:

3/5 and 3/7; 2/7 and 2/3; 1/4 and 1/2; 5/7 and 5/9

3/5 > 3/7; 2/7 < 2/3; 1/4 < 1/2; 5/7 > 5/9

FR1-107 Arrange the fractions in order, beginning with the smallest:

2/3 2/5 2/11 2/7 2/4

The smallest fraction will have the greatest denominator (all the numerators are equal):

2/11 2/7 2/5 2/4 2/3

FR1-108 Josh won today a math contest and his mom doubled his allowance to $6 a week. What was his allowance last week?

Half of 6 is 3. His allowance last week was $3.

FR1-109 Arrange the fractions in order, beginning with the greatest:

5/6 5/11 5/7 5/9 5/12

The greatest fraction will have the smallest denominator (all the numerators are equal):

5/6 5/7 5/9 5/11 5/12

FR1-110 Compare the following fractions:

4/7 and 4/5; 5/9 and 5/7; 7/8 and 7/11

4/7 < 4/5; 5/9 < 5/7; 7/8 > 7/11

FR1-111 Maria got 10 apples from her grandma. She gave half of them to her friend, Ann. How many apples did Ann get?

Half of 10 is 5. Ann got 5 apples.

FR1-112 John has 48 black and white Lego pieces. Half of them are black. How many white Lego pieces does he have?

If half of the pieces are black, then the other half are white. Half of 48 is 24. John has 24 white pieces.

Level 2

FR2-116 Min returned 1/5 of the books that he checked out from the public library last week. He is planning to read the remaining 8 books by the end of the week. How many books did he check out?

The total number of cards (we don't know how many):

Min returned 1/5 of the books. Let's divide the entire number of books in 5 groups:

1/5	1/5	1/5	1/5	1/5

After he returned 1/5 of the books, he had 8 books left to read by the end of the week:

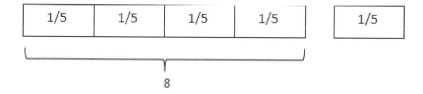

How much would 1/5 be? We have to divide 8 in 4 equal parts. The students can use trial and error if they are not comfortable with the division yet.

2 + 2 + 2 + 2 = 8, so 1/5 of the books is 2.

To get the total number of books checked out, we add all the 5 individual parts together:

2 + 2 + 2 + 2 + 2 = 10

Answer: Min checked out 10 books.

FR2-117 Vlad has a collection of 30 stones. 1/5 of them are quartz minerals, 1/6 of them are lava stones, and the rest of them are Petoskey stones. How many Petoskey stones does Vlad have?

What is 1/5 out of 30 stones? Use the Sticky Method. Divide the whole group in groups of 5 and then circle one stick in every group:

1/5 of 30 stones is 6. Vlad had 6 quartz minerals.

What is 1/6 out of 30 stones? Use the Sticky Method. Divide the whole group in groups of 6 and then circle one stick in every group:

1/6 of 30 stones is 5. Vlad had 5 lava stones.

The rest of the stones are Petoskey stones:

30 − 6 − 5 = 19. **Answer:** Vlad has 19 Petoskey stones.

FR2-118 Stony Creek Farm has 18 bunnies. 1/6 of them are white and the rest of them are black. How many black bunnies are there?

Again, use the Sticky Method:

1/6 of 18 is 3. So there are 3 white bunnies and the rest of them are black:

18 − 3 = 15

Answer: There 15 black bunnies in the Stony Creek Farm.

FR2-119 Gene's mom got back from the farmer's market with 24 fruits. 1/2 of them were apples, 1/4 were peaches, 1/6 of them were plums. The rest of the fruits were pears. How many pears did she buy?

1/2 of 24 = 12 apples– The students should know this by now without any help

1/4 of 24 = 6 peaches– See **FR2-113**

1/6 of 24 = 4 plums:

The total number of apples, peaches, and plums is 12 + 6 + 4 = 22

The rest of the fruits: 24 − 22 = 2

Answer: Gene's mom bought 2 pears.

FR2-120 After John gave Sydney 1/4 of his stamps collection, he still had 21 stamps left. How many stamps did John have initially?

The total number of stamps (we don't know how many):

John gave Sydney 1/4 of the stamps. Let's divide the entire number of books in 4 groups:

| 1/4 | 1/4 | 1/4 | 1/4 |

After he gave Sydney 1/4 of the books, he had 21 left:

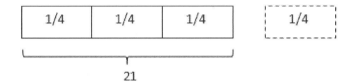

How much would 1/4 be? We have to divide 21 in 3 equal parts. The students can use trial and error if they are not comfortable with the division yet.

7 + 7 + 7 = 21, so 1/4 of the stamps is 7.

To get the total initial number of stamps, we add all the 4 individual parts together:

7 + 7 + 7 + 7 = 28

Answer: John had initially 28 stamps in his collection.

FR2-121 There are 24 students in Mrs. Mustola class. 1/3 of them are boys. How many girls are there?

Use the Sticky Method to find 1/3 of 24:

Count the circles: 8. So 1/3 of 24 is 8.

The number of girls: 24 − 8 = 16 girls

FR2-122 Trenton uses a bucket with 100 tennis balls in his daily training. Today he's going to practice his serve with 1/4 of the ball and his backhand shot with 1/10 of the balls. He'll use the rest of the balls to practice his forehand shot. How many balls will he use for his forehand?

Well, we are not going to draw 100 sticks for the Sticky Method. Instead, the students should make an analogy with the money.

1 dollar is 100 cents.

1/4 of a dollar is a quarter and we all know that is 25 cents.

1/10 of a dollar is a dime and we know that is 10 cents.

So Trenton uses 25 balls to practice his serve and 10 balls for his backhand shot.

25 +10 = 35.

Trenton uses the rest of the balls for forehand: 100 − 35 = 65 balls.

Level 3

FR3-125. Joe has $25 to spend at the fair. He gives two fifths of his money to his friend who didn't have any, and then he spent two thirds of the remaining money on games. After that he wanted to eat a hamburger that cost $4.99. Does he have enough money to buy the hamburger?

2/5 of $25 = $10:

Remaining money: 25 – 10 = $15

He spends 2/3 of the remaining money on games. 2/3 of $15 = $10:

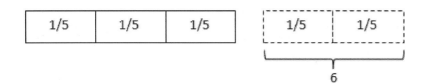

Remaining money: 15 – 10 = $5. The hamburger costs $4.99, so , the answer is yes, Joe has enogh money to buy it.

FR3-126. Vlad has just started a collection of Discovery magazines. He collected 6 magazines – that's only 2/5 of his neighbor's collection. How many magazines does his neighbor have?

The total number of magazines collected by Vlad's neighbor (we don't know how many):

Vlad has 2/5 of his neighbor's magazines. Let's divide the entire number of magazines in 5 groups:

| 1/5 | 1/5 | 1/5 | 1/5 | 1/5 |

Vlad collected 6 magazines and that is 2/5 of his neighbor's magazines:

| 1/5 | 1/5 | 1/5 | | 1/5 | 1/5 |

6

How much would 1/5 be? We have to divide 6 in 2 equal parts.

3 + 3 = 6, so 1/5 of the Vlad's neighbor magazines is 3.

To get the total number of magazines collected by the neighbor, we add all the 5 individual parts together:

3 + 3 + 3 + 3 + 3 = 15

Answer: Vlad's neighbor has 15 magazines.

FR3-127. There are 32 students in Mrs. Mustola's class. Three fourths of them like to read in the Free Choice hour. Three fourths of the remaining students like to draw. The rest of the students paint. How many students paint?

Use the Sticky Method to find 3/4 of 32. Divide the sticks in groups of 4 and then circle 3 sticks in each group:

000 | 000 | 000 | 000 | 000 | 000 | 000 | 000 |

Count the circled sticks. 3/4 of 32 is 24 students.

The remaining students: 32 − 24 = 8 students

Use the same method to find 3/4 of 8:

000 | 000 |

3/4 of 8 is 6.

The rest of the students paint. We calculate again the remaining students: 8 − 6 = 2 students.

Answer: 2 students like to paint.

FR3-128. Sydney has 18 Magic Tree House books. She wants to trade 5/6 of them for some Ramona books. How many Magic Tree House books will she have left?

Use the Sticky Method to find that 5/6 of 18 is 15:

00000 | 00000 | 00000 |

So Sydney wants to trade 15 Magic Tree House books for some Ramona books. Let's see how many she'll have left:

18 − 15 = 3 books

Answer: Sydney will have 3 books left.

FR3-129. Gene's soccer practice is 1 hour and a half. He spends 1/3 of that for warm-up, 1/2 of the remaining time for speed drills. He practices his goal shot for the rest of the time. He shots 2 times every minute. How many shots does he do?

The easiest way to solve this problem is to work with half hours. 1 hour has 2 half hours, so 1 hour and a half is the same with 3 half hours:

So Gene spends 30 minutes to practice his shot on goal. He shots 2 times a minute.

2 x 30 = 30 + 30 = 60 shots

Answer: Gene does 60 shots on goal as part of his soccer practice.

FR3-130. One large pizza usually feeds 4 people. How many people will 2 and a half pizzas feed?

If one pizza feeds 4 people, then a half of pizza feeds 2 people.

1 pizza feeds 4 people
1 pizza feeds 4 people
1/2 pizza feeds 2 people

Two and a half pizza feed 4 + 4 + 2 = 10 people

Answer: 10 people

FR3-131. A sack of oat will feed 4 horses. How many horses will two and a half sacks feed?

If one sack feeds 4 horses, then a half of sack feeds 2 horses.

1 sack feeds 4 horses
1 sack feeds 4 horses

1/2 sack feeds 2 horses

Two and a half sacks feed 4 + 4 + 2 = 10 horses

Answer: 10 horses

FR3-132. Dan's grandma usually uses two and half cups of flour to bake 30 cookies. But today she only wants to bake 15 cookies. How much flour would she need?

$2\frac{1}{2}$ cups $\longrightarrow$ 30 cookies

The students should be able to figure that 15 is actually half of 30. So grandma should use half of the flour to bake 15 cookies. Half of 2 cups is 1 cup, and half of 1/2 cup is 1/4.

$1\frac{1}{4}$ cups $\longrightarrow$ 15 cookies

Three Little Birds

LB-133. Dan is in the 3rd grade now and he would like to donate his Kindergarten books. He gives 3/7 of his books to his cousin, and a half of the remaining ones to his neighbor. He still has 6 remaining books and he's thinking to donate them to the Public Library. How many books did Dan initially have?

The total number of Kindergarten books (we don't know how many):

He gives 3/7 of his books to his cousin. Let's divide the entire number of books in 7 equal groups:

| 1/7 | 1/7 | 1/7 | 1/7 | 1/7 | 1/7 | 1/7 |

3/7 of the books go to Dan's cousin:

| 1/7 | 1/7 | 1/7 | 1/7 | | 1/7 | 1/7 | 1/7 |

Half of the remaining ones go to his neighbor, and then he is left with 6 books:

6

We now divide 6 in 2 equal parts to find out what 1/7 is.

3 + 3 = 6, so 1/7 of the books is 3.

To get the total number of books that Dan initially had, we add all the 7 individual parts together:

3 + 3 + 3 + 3 + 3 + 3 + 3 = 21

Answer: Dan had initially 21 books.

LB-134. Trenton and Gene collect postage stamps. Trenton has 21 stamps and gave Gene 6 stamps to have both the same number. How many did Gene have initially?

Trenton has 21 stamps and he gives Gene 6 stamps.

Trenton has now 21 -6 = 15 stamps, the same as Gene.

Gene received 6 stamps from Trenton, so he had before 15 – 6 = 9 stamps.

Answer: Gene had 9 stamps initially.

LB-135. The sum of 2 numbers is 12. Their difference is 10. What is the largest number?

Don't even think to try system of equations. The only way the second graders can easily solve such problems is through trial and error:

N1 + N2 = 12

N1 – N2 = 10

We'll just pick to numbers whose sum is 12. Let's say 8 and 4:

N1	N2	N1 + N2	N1 – N2	Correct?
8	4	12	4	No
10	2	12	8	No
11	1	12	10	Yes

Answer: The largest number is 11.

Angry Bird

AB-136. A large loaf of bread will last two and a half days for Pete and his parents. How long will the loaf last for the parents when Pete goes in summer camp (presuming that all 3 of them eat the same quantity of bread)?

This problem is probably a little bit too difficult for a second grader, but, hey, this is an angry bird, isn't it? Let's go step by step:

3 people finish a load of bread in two and half days:

→ 2 $\frac{1}{2}$ days

How long will it take for one person to finish that loaf? Let's say one person eats alone from the loaf for two and half days. He would still have the portion that the other 2 would have eaten. If he goes on and he eats from the bread for another two and a half days, he would still have the portion that the third person would have eaten. So one person can eat from the loaf for as long as 3 periods of two and half days, that is 7 days and half:

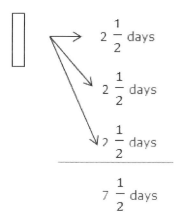

2 $\frac{1}{2}$ days

2 $\frac{1}{2}$ days

2 $\frac{1}{2}$ days

7 $\frac{1}{2}$ days

Now that we know how long a loaf of bread lasts for one person, we have to find out how long it will last for 2 persons (Peter's parents). The answer now is clear: the loaf will last for 2 persons half the time it lasted for one person. It gets a little more complicated when we calculate that.

Half of 7 → $3\frac{1}{2}$ or $3\frac{2}{4}$ or 3 and 2 quarters

Half of $\frac{1}{2}$ → $\frac{1}{4}$ or 1 quarter

Half of 7 $\frac{1}{2}$ → $3\frac{3}{4}$ or 3 and 3 quarters

So the loaf will last 3 and 3/4 days for Peter's parents while he's in summer camp:

→ 3 $\frac{3}{4}$ days

Week 5

Level 1

OL01-141. Put the following sums in ascending order: 12+14, 18+17, 19+27, 28+3

12+14 = 26, 18+17 = 35, 19+27 = 46, 28+3 = 31

1st	2nd	3rd	4th
26	31	35	46

OL01-142. Put the following sums in descending order: 37+15, 48+17, 39+28, 27+15, 56-17

37+15 = 52, 48+17 = 65, 39+28 = 67, 27+15 = 42, 56-17 = 39

1st	2nd	3rd	4th	5th
67	65	52	42	39

OL01-143. What is the median value of the following set of numbers: 47, 59, 23, 51, 76?

Put the number in order and then pick the middle value:

1st	2nd	3rd	4th	5th
23	51		47	76

OL01-144. What is the median value and the modal in the following set of numbers: 22-5, 11+6, 7+5, 6+5, 19+13, 13+8, 14+9?

Solve the number sentences:

22-5 = 17, 11+6 = 17, 7+5 = 12, 6+5 = 11, 19+13 = 32, 13+8 = 22, 14+9 = 23

Write the results in order:

1st	2nd	3rd	4th	5th	6th	7th
11	12	17		22	23	32

Pick the middle value:

Median Value: 17

Pick the most frequent number:

Modal Value: 17 (shows up 2 times)

OL01-145. What is the median value and the modal in the following set of numbers: 12+4, 22-6, 22-11, 6+5, 9+2, 13-8, 14-9?

Solve the number sentences:

12+4 = 16, 22-6 = 16, 22-11 = 11, 6+5 = 11, 9+2 = 11, 13-8 = 5, 14-9 = 5

Write the results in order:

1st	2nd	3rd	4th	5th	6th	7th
5	5	11		11	16	16

Pick the middle value:

Medial Value: 11

Pick the most frequent number:

Modal Value: 11 (shows up 3 times)

OL01-146. What is the median value and the modal in the following set of numbers: 18+3, 12+7, 24 -5, 6+6, 9+14, 23-8, 14+9?

Solve the number sentences:

18+3 = 21, 12+7 = 19, 24 -5 = 19, 6+6 = 12, 9+14 = 23, 23-8 = 15, 14+9 = 23

Write the results in order:

1st	2nd	3rd	4th	5th	6th	7th
12	15	19	19	21	23	23

Pick the middle value:

Medial Value: 19

Pick the most frequent number:

Modal Values: 19, 23 (both numbers show up 2 times)

Level 2

OL02-149. Mike has 5 shirts: 2 yellow and 3 blue. He arranges them in 3 drawers:
1 yellow shirt in the bottom drawer
1 yellow shirt in the middle drawer
Every shirt in the middle drawer is yellow
There are no blue shirts in the bottom drawer
How many shirts are in the top drawer?

Solution:
Mike had 5 shirts: Y Y B B B

B B B
Y
Y

There are no blue shirts in the bottom or the middle drawers. So all of them are in top drawer. And since the rest of the shirts (2 yellow shirts) is in the bottom and middle drawer, then there are 3 shirts in the top drawer.

OL02-150. Jack, Don, and Mike are three penguins who like to go fishing together. They walk one by one in line. Don and Mike never like to end the line. Jack never likes to lead. Don feels cold most of the time and prefers to walk in the middle, to avoid the wind. Who is leading the group?

Don and Mike never like to end the line. Let's cross them out:

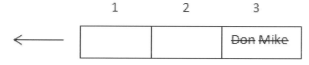

Jack never likes to lead:

Don walks in the middle:

Since Don and Mike don't like to end the line, then Jack must do it. Don is in the middle, so Mike will have to lead the group:

OL02-151 Vlad's toy train has 5 cars: white, blue, yellow, green, and red. There are 2 cars in front of the yellow car, and 3 cars in front of the green car. The red car is the caboose. The white car is not in front of the train. What car do you think Vlad will place in front?

There are 2 cars in front of the yellow car, and 3 cars in front of the green car:

The red car is the caboose:

The white car is not in front of the train, so it must be the second. Then the blue car can only be the first:

OL02-152 Sydney, Daria, and Mary stand in line at the ice-cream shop. Sydney is not the first. Mary is the last in line. Daria is not in the middle. Who is going to get ice-cream first?

Sydney is not the first

Mary is the last

Daria is not in the middle

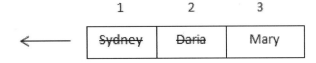

So Daria must be first in line and Sydney the second:

OL02-153 Jack, Marvin, and Min stand in line to get on the bus. Jack always waits until everyone else got on the bus. Marvin doesn't like to be the first, and Min doesn't like to stand in the middle. In what order do they get on the bus?

Jack is the last in line

Marvin is not the first

Min is not in the middle

So Min is first in line and Marvin the second:

OL02-154 A group of kids stand in line in the ice-cream store. Mary is third in line counting from the beginning of the line and fourth counting from the end of the line. How many kids are in line?

Mary is the third in line counting from the beginning of the line:

| | M

She's also the forth in line counting from the end of the line:

M | | |

So there are 7 kids in the line:

| | M | | |

OL02-155 Trenton has 5 shirts: 2 yellow, 2 white, and 1 blue. He arranges them in 3 drawers: There is 1 yellow shirt in the middle drawer and 1 white shirt in the top drawer. There are only 2 shirts in the middle drawer and only 1 shirt in the bottom drawer. The blue shirt is not in the top or middle drawers. What shirts does Trenton have in each drawer?

There is 1 yellow shirt in the middle drawer and 1 white shirt in the top drawer.

There are only 2 shirts in the middle drawer and only 1 shirt in the bottom drawer:

W
Y ?
?

That means the fifth shirt is in the top drawer. The blue shirt is not in the top or middle drawers, so it has to be in the bottom drawer:

W ?
Y ?
B

There is only one shirt in the middle drawer, so the other one has to be white.

There is only one shirt in the top drawer, so the other one has to be yellow:

W Y
Y W
B

OL02-156 Sydney, Vlad, Trenton, and Gene are waiting in line at the library to check out their books. The boys let Sydney to be the first in line. Gene is behind Trenton and Vlad is not the last in the line. In what order do they stand in line?

Sydney is the first in line and Vlad is not the last:

← | Sydney | | | ~~Vlad~~ |

Gene is behind Trenton so they need 2 sequential spots. Since Vlad is not the last in the line, he will have to stand right after Sydney to allow Gene and Trenton to stand one next to the other:

← | Sydney | Vlad | Trenton | Gene |

Level 3

OL03-160. Linda, Greg, Calvin and John are the only four people standing in a line. John is not standing next to either Linda or Calvin. Calvin is the first one in line. Who is the second person in line?

Calvin is the first in line. John is not standing next to Calvin, so he can't be in the second position.

1st	2nd	3rd	4th
Calvin	~~John~~		

John can't stand in the 3rd position either, because he would stand between Greg and Linda, and he can't stand next to Linda. So John is the last in line.

1st	2nd	3rd	4th
Calvin	Linda	Greg	John

Linda has to stay away from John, so she is the second in line.

Answer: Linda is the second person in line.

OL03-161. Twenty children sit in a row watching a carols concert. Leila is the 14th child from one end of the line. Diane is the 16th child from the other end of the line. How many children are between Leila and Diane?

We just need to sketch how the kids would be lined up:

| | | | | | | | | | | | | L | | | | | | |

We can see that there are 8 kids between Leila and Diane.

We can get to the same result by following a **different solution**:

How many kids are there to the right of Leila: 20-14=6
How many kids are there to the left of Diane: 20-16=4

So the number of children between Leila and Diane is

Kids Between = (Total number) − (Kids to the right of Leila) − (Kids to the left of Diane) − Leila − Diane = 20 − 6 − 4 − 1 − 1 = 8

The second solution works better for big numbers (what if we had 1,000 kids sitting in a row?)

Answer: There are 8 children between Leila and Diane.

OL03-162. A group of kids stand in line in the ice-cream store. Mary is third in line counting from beginning of the line. Diane is the fifth in line counting from the end of the line. There are 3 more kids between Mary and Diane. How many kids are in the line?

Mary is third in line counting from beginning of the line:

| | M

Diane is the fifth in line counting from the end of the line:

D | | | |

There are 3 more kids between Mary and Diane:

| | M | | | D | | | |

There are 11 kids in the line.

OL03-163. Greg, Jack, Maia and John are all different heights. Greg and Jack are neither the tallest nor the shortest. Maia is shorter than Jack and John. Who is the tallest kid?

Don't try to find the order of their heights. Just focus on the question – who is the tallest kid?

Neither Greg nor Jack is the tallest.

Mary is shorter than Jack and John, so she's definitely not the tallest.

The only remaining kid is John, who has to be the tallest.

Answer: John is the tallest kid.

OL03-164 Five cars wait at the traffic light, one behind the other. There are 3 cars in front of the yellow car, and 1 car in front of the red car. The blue car is right in front of the traffic light. The white car is not the last. Where is remaining green car?

Three cars in front of the yellow car and 1 car in front of the red car:

The blue car is the first and the white car is not the last:

The white car must be in the middle because that the only spot available. Then the remaining green car is the last:

OL03-165 Mark, Vincent, Cory and TJ are all different heights. Vincent and Cory are neither the tallest nor the shortest. TJ is shorter than Vincent and Mark. In how many ways can we arrange them in the order of their heights?

This problem is similar with problem OL03-163, but is one notch more difficult.

Neither Vincent nor Cory is the tallest.

TJ is shorter than Vincent and Mark, so TJ is not the tallest. The only remaining kid is Mark, who has to be the tallest:

Neither Vincent nor Cory is the tallest, so they will share the 2nd and 3rd place among them. That means TJ is the shortest. We don't have any information about which spot will be taken by each of Vincent and Cory. So we have the following options:

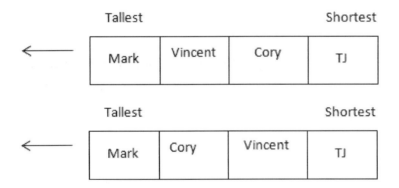

Answer: We can arrange them in 2 ways.

OL03-166 Olivia, Jen, Sydney and Delilah are the only 4 girls standing in a line. Sydney is not standing next to either Olivia or Jen. Jen is the last in line. In what order do they stand in line?

The only thing that we know for sure is the Jen is the last in line. And since Sydney is not standing next to either Olivia or Jen, she can't stand in the third position:

Sydney is not the second in line either, because she would stand between Olivia and Delilah, and she can't stand next to Olivia. So Sydney must stand first in line and Delilah is second:

Three Little Birds

LB-167. Vlad goes on bike race. There are 2 water stops during the race where Vlad can stop and fill his water bottle. The distance between the start point and the first water stop is 7 miles. The distance between the first water stop and the finish line is 8 miles. The distance between the second water stop and the finish line is 5 miles. What is the distance between the start line and the second water stop?

The very first thing we have to do is make a drawing. It is always easy to have a picture of the problem:

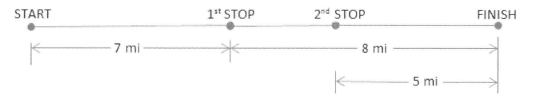

We have to find the distance between START and 2nd STOP. This distance is made up of 2 smaller distances:

- The distance between START and 1st STOP (7 miles)
- The distance between 1st STOP and 2nd STOP (**unknown**)

We know that the distance between 1st STOP and FINISH is 8 miles, and the distance between the 2nd STOP and FINISH and 5 miles. If we look at the drawing, we see that we can subtract these 2 distances to find the distance between 1st STOP and 2nd STOP: $8 - 5 = 3$ miles

We go back and replace the **unknown**:

The distance between START and 2nd STOP =

The distance between START and 1st STOP (7 miles) + The distance between 1st STOP and 2nd STOP (**3 miles**) = $7 + 3 = 10$ miles

Answer: The distance between START and 2nd STOP is 10 miles.

LB-168. Find the value of A, if $59 + A = 65 - A$.

Trial and Error:

A=1: $59+1 = 65-1$? No, $60 \neq 64$

A=3: $59 + 3 = 65 - 3$? Yes, $62 = 62$

Answer: A = 3

LB-169. Vlad has 18 cookies. He eats either 2 cookie or 3 cookies a day.
Question 1: At least how many days will the cookies last?
Question 2: At most how many days will the cookies last?

Question 1. The cookies will last a **minimum number (at least)** of days if Vlad eats as **many** as possible every day – that is 3 cookies a day.

Day 1 – 3 cookies, Day 2 – 6 cookies, Day 3 – 9 cookies, Day 4 – 12 cookies, Day 5 – 15 cookies, Day 6 – 18 cookies. Stop.

Answer 1: The cookies will last at least 6 days

Question 2. The cookies will last a **maximum number (at most)** of days if Vlad eats as **few** as possible every day – that is 2 cookies a day.

Day 1 – 2 cookies, Day 2 – 4 cookies, Day 3 – 6 cookies, Day 4 – 8 cookies, Day 5 – 10 cookies, Day 6 – 12 cookies, Day 7 – 14 cookies, Day 8 – 16 cookies, Day 9 – 18 cookies. Stop.

Answer 2: The cookies will last at most 9 days

Angry Bird

AB-170. The teacher brings a jar with marbles in the classroom. There are 7 red marbles, 5 yellow marbles and 2 blue marbles in the jar. The teacher blindfolds Gene and asks him to draw marbles from the jar.
1. How many marbles does Gene have to draw to be sure that he draws at least one red marble?
2. How many marbles does Gene have to draw to be sure that he draws at least one blue marble?
3. How many marbles does Gene have to draw to be sure that he draws at least one yellow marble?
4. How many marbles does Gene have to draw to be sure that he draws at least one marble of each color?

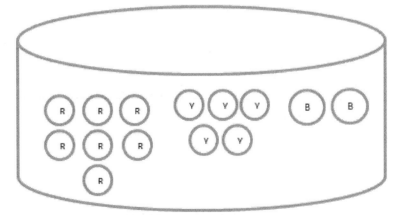

1. Remember – Gene is blindfolded; he can't see the marbles that he draws out of the jar.

He has to draw at least one red marble. Let's suppose that he is a very unlucky guy and he draws all the yellow and blue marbles first. So in the worst case, he will extract 5 + 2 = 7 marbles before starting to draw the first **red** marble. That means he has to draw 8 marbles to make sure at least one of them is red.

Answer: 8 marbles

2. We'll apply the same logic:

In the worst case, he will have to extract all the red and yellow marbles before drawing the first **blue** marble: 7 + 5 +1 = 13

Answer: 13 marbles

3. Again:

In the worst case, he will have to extract all the red and yellow marbles before drawing the first **yellow** marble: 7 + 2 +1 = 10

Answer: 13 marbles

4. Gene may very well draw all the red marbles (the greatest number of marbles having the same color) and all the yellow marbles (the second greatest number of marbles having the same color) before drawing a blue marble.

So he has to extract 7+5+1=13 marbles to make sure he gets at least one marble of each color.

Answer: 13 marbles

Week 6

Level 1

IM1-173 Vlad bought 6 Lego figures. Each figure cost $4. How much did Vlad pay altogether?

Each of the 6 Lego figures costs $4: 4 + 4 + 4 + 4 + 4 + 4 = 24

[6] × [4] = [24]

IM1-174 Sydney bought 5 boxes of cookies. There are 6 cookies in each box. How many cookies did he buy altogether?

5 boxes with 6 cookies in each box: 6 + 6 + 6 + 6 + 6 = 30

IM1-175 Daria prepared 3 pots of tea. She used 6 cubes of sugar for each pot of tea. How many cubes of sugar did she use altogether?

3 pots of tea with 6 cubes of sugar in each of them: 6 + 6 + 6 = 18

IM1-176 Vlad spent $2 a week on bagels. How much did he spend in 6 weeks?

$2 a week for 6 weeks: $2 + $2 + $2 + $2 + $2 + $2 = $12

IM1-177 John bought 9 pieces of rope. Each piece was 3 meters long. How many meters of rope did John buy?

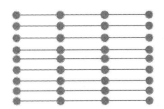

It is important for the student to realize that rather than adding 3 meters 9 times, they can do 9 + 9 + 9, with the same result. It is easier.

Answer: John bought 27 meters of rope.

IM1-178 There are 5 roses planted in a row. How many roses are there in 7 rows?

7 + 7 + 7 + 7 + 7 = 35

5 × 7 = 35

IM1-179 A book costs $10. Mrs. Johns sold 11 copies of the book. How much money did she receive?

10 + 10 + 10 + 10 + 10 + 10 + 10 + 10 + 10 + 10 + 10 = $110

10 × 11 = 110

IM1-180 David found 5 nests with 7 eggs in each of them. How many eggs did he find?

7 + 7 + 7 + 7 + 7 = 35

| 5 | × | 7 | = | 35 |

Level 2

IM2-183 Donna had 17 stickers. She gave three stickers to each of her four friends. How many stickers does she have left?

Three stickers for 4 friends: 3 + 3 + 3 + 3 = 12

17 − 12 = 5 - So Donna still has 5 stickers left.

Number Sentence: 17 - 3 x 4 = 5   (the teacher can briefly discuss about the operations precedence)

IM2-184 Gene earns a star for every 6 problems he solves. He solved 45 problems until today. How many stars did Gene earn?

6 + 6 = 12 –less than 45

6 + 6 + 6 = 18 –less than 45

6 + 6 + 6 + 6 = 24 –less than 45

6 + 6 + 6 + 6 + 6 = 30 –less than 45

6 + 6 + 6 + 6 + 6 + 6 = 36 –less than 45

6 + 6 + 6 + 6 + 6 + 6 + 6 = 42 –less than 45

6 + 6 + 6 + 6 + 6 + 6 + 6 + 6 = 48 –greater than 45 – STOP! Go back a line and count all the 6s.

There are 7 6s, so Gene got 7 stars.

Number sentence: 6 x 7 + 3 = 45

IM2-185 There are 5 pigs and some chickens in the barn. The chickens and the pigs have 30 legs altogether. How many chickens are there in the barn?

One pig has 4 legs, so 5 pigs will have 4 + 4 + 4 + 4 +4 = 5 x 4 = 20 legs

The remaining legs belong to the chickens: 30 − 20 = 10 legs. How many chickens?

2 + 2 + 2 + 2 + 2 = 10

Answer: 5 chickens

IM2-186 There are 5 bicycles and 3 tricycles left in Rochester Bike Store. How many wheels are there altogether?

5 bicycles have 2 + 2 + 2 + 2 +2 = 10 wheels

3 tricycles have 3 + 3 + 3 = 9 wheels

There are 10 + 9 = 19 wheels altogether.

5 X 2 + 3 X 3 = 19

IM2-187 Gene has 7 dozens of crayons. He gives Trenton 3 dozens. How many crayons does Gene have now?

Gene has 7 – 3 = 4 dozens.

12 + 12 + 12 + 12 = 48 crayons.

(7 – 3) X 12 = 48

IM2-188 The pigs in the barn have all 22 eyes. How many legs do they have?

22 eyes are 11 pairs of eyes. So there 11 pigs in the barn. They all have

11 + 11 + 11 + 11 = 44 legs

11 x 4 = 44

IM2-189 An apple costs $0.25 and a pineapple costs $1.5. Sydney bought 5 apples and 3 pineapples. How much did she pay?

5 apples cost 0.25 + 0.25 + 0.25 + 0.25 + 0.25 = $1.25

3 pineapples cost 1.5 + 1.5 + 1.5 = $4.5

Sydney paid 1.25 + 4.5 = $5.75

5 X 0.25 + 3 X 1.5 = $5.75

IM2-190 Josh needs 30 paint brushes for a project. He went to Home Depot and found boxes with 8 brushes. How many boxes did he have to buy?

8 + 8 = 16 –less than 30

8 + 8 + 8 = 24 –less than 30

8 + 8 + 8 + 8 = 32 –more than 30 - STOP

Josh has to by 4 boxes.

30 = 4 X 8 - 2

Level 3

IM3-193 Vlad brings home 12 pencils every day from Owl's Nest. He arranges them in boxes of 10 pencils each. He does that until he has only boxes with 10 pencils. How many boxes does he have?

$12 + 12 = 24 = 2 \times 10 + 4$ — the 3rd box has only 4 pencils

$12 + 12 + 12 = 36 = 3 \times 10 + 6$ — the 4th box has only 6 pencils

$12 + 12 + 12 + 12 = 48 = 4 \times 10 + 8$ — the 5th box had only 8 pencils

$12 + 12 + 12 + 12 + 12 = 60 = 6 \times 10$ — all the pencils fit in 6 boxes

Answer: 6 boxes

IM3-194 There were 58 people at Gene's party. 5 kids came with both their parents and one grandparent, 7 kids came with both parents, and 8 kids came with only one parent. How many kids came alone at the party?

5 kids came with both their parents and one grandparent: ⟶ $5 + 5 + 5 + 5 = 20$ people

7 kids came with both parents: ⟶ $7 + 7 + 7 = 21$ people

8 kids came with only one parent: ⟶ $8 + 8 = 16$ people

Total: $20 + 21 + 16 = 57$ people

The rest of the people were kids who cam alone to the party: $58 - 57 = 1$ kid

Number sentence: $58 - (5 \times 4) - (7 \times 3) - (8 \times 2) = 1$

Answer: 1 kid

IM3-195 In the Paintcreek Golf Club's parking lot there are golf carts with 6 wheels and 8 wheels. The total number of wheels is 70. The number of 6-wheel carts is the same as the number of 8-wheel carts. How many 6-wheel carts are in the parking lot?

Trial and Error:

Carts with 6 wheels	Carts with 8 wheels	Total number of wheels	Correct answer?
1	1	$1 \times 6 + 1 \times 8 = 14$	No
2	2	$2 \times 6 + 2 \times 8 = 28$	No
3	3	$3 \times 6 + 3 \times 8 = 42$	No
4	4	$4 \times 6 + 4 \times 8 = 56$	No
5	5	$5 \times 6 + 5 \times 8 = 70$	Yes!!

Answer: There are 5 6-wheel carts in the parking lot.

IM3-196 In Mrs. Jones' class there are 5 desks. 4 students sit on every desk and every student has 3 books. How many books are in Mrs. Jones' class?

Desk 1: Student 1 – **3 books**;   Student 2 – **3 books**;   Student 3 – **3 books**;   Student 4 – **3 books**

Desk 2: Student 1 – **3 books**;   Student 2 – **3 books**;   Student 3 – **3 books**;   Student 4 – **3 books**

Desk 3: Student 1 – **3 books**;   Student 2 – **3 books**;   Student 3 – **3 books**;   Student 4 – **3 books**

Desk 4: Student 1 – **3 books**;   Student 2 – **3 books**;   Student 3 – **3 books**;   Student 4 – **3 books**

Desk 5: Student 1 – **3 books**;   Student 2 – **3 books**;   Student 3 – **3 books**;   Student 4 – **3 books**

There are 3 + 3 + 3 + 3 = 12 books on every desk.

There are 12 + 12 + 12 + 12 + 12 + 12 = 60 books on all 5 desks.

Number sentence: 4 x 3 x 5 = 60 books

IM3-197 Two 2nd grade classes went on a field trip to Dinosaur Hill. Each class had 11 students, 1 teacher, 1 para-professional, and 1 parent. How many people went on a field trip?

Each class has 11 + 1 + 1 +1 = 14 people.

There are 14 + 14 = 28 people in 2 classes.

Number sentence: 2 X (11 + 1 + 1 + 1) = 28 people

IM3-198 22 kids showed up at Vlad's birthday party. He had 3 dozens of cookies and wanted to offer each kid 2 cookies. How many more cookies did he need?

Vlad wants to offer each of the 22 kids 2 cookies – that is 22 + 22 = 44 cookies.

3 dozens of cookies are 12 + 12 + 12 = 36 cookies.

Vlad need 44 – 36 = 8 more cookies (see More or Less problems).

Number sentence: (22 X 2) – (12 X 3) = 8

IM3-199. Jeff keeps his collection of Ninjago in his room. He has 4 Ninjagos in each of the 5 shelves and 3 other Ninjagos in each of the 4 boxes under his bed. How many Ninjago does Jeff have?

5 shelves with 4 Ninjagos in each of them: 4 + 4 + 4 + 4 + 4 = 20

4 boxes with 3 Ninjagos in each of them: 4 + 4 + 4 = 12

Jeff has 20 + 12 = 32 Ninjagos

Number sentence: (4 x 5) + (4 x 3) = 32

IM3-200. There are 3 times as many pigs as chickens in a barn. There are 42 legs altogether. How many chickens are in the barn?

Trial and error:

Number of chickens	Number of pigs	Total number of legs	Correct answer?
1	3	1 x 2 + 3 x 4 = 14	No
2	6	2 x 2 + 6 x 4 = 28	No
3	9	3 x 2 + 9 x 4 = 42	Yes!!

Answer: There are 3 chickens in the barn.

Three Little Birds

LB-201 Sleepy is taller than Doc by as much as Doc is taller than Happy. Sleepy is 3'3" tall and Doc is 2'9" tall. How tall is Happy?

Here's the drawing:

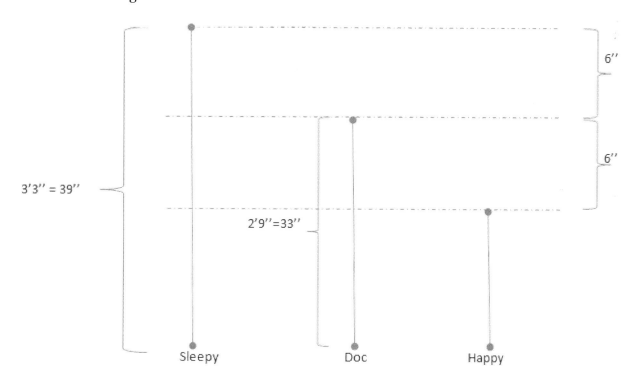

Sleepy is 39 – 33 = 6" taller than Doc

Since Sleepy is taller than Doc by as much as Doc is taller than Happy, then Doc is 6" taller than Happy.

So Happy is 33 – 6 = 27", which is 2' 3 " (2 feet and 3 inches)

LB-202 John paid for 5 pencils with 4 quarters, 4 dimes, 2 nickels. The following day he needed to buy 10 more pencils for his friend. He only had 3 quarters and 3 dimes. How much more did he need?

John paid for 5 pencils with 4 quarters, 4 dimes, 2 nickels – that is $1.50

He will have to pay double for 10 pencils – that is $3.00

He had 3 quarters and 3 dimes – that is $1.05

So John needed $3.00 - $1.05 = $1.95 more money to buy the 10 pencils for his friend.

Answer: $1.95

LB-203 What number must be added to the sum of 18 and 17 to equal the sum of 15 and 27?

$18 + 17 + ? = 15 + 27$ $\qquad$ $35 + ? = 42$ $\qquad$ $? = 42 - 35 = 7$

Answer: 7

Angry Bird

AB_204 Sam likes to raise rabbits in his farm. The difference between the total number of their legs and the total number of their tails is 30. A rabbit eats 2 carrots every day. How many carrots does Sam need to feed all the rabbits for an entire week?

Start with trial and error:

Number of Rabbits	Difference between total number of legs and total number of tails
1	4-1 = 3
2	8-2 = 6
3	12 – 3 = 9
See the pattern? Count by 3 until 30 and see how many rabbits Sam has.	
4	12
5	15
6	18
7	21
8	24
9	27
10	30

So Sam has 10 rabbits. They eat 10 X 2 = 20 carrots every day. Sam needs to have 20 X 7 = 140 carrots to feed the rabbits for a week.

Answer: 140 carrots

Week 7

Level 1

ID1-207 Vlad paid $24 for 6 Lego figures. How much was one figure?

Each of the 6 Lego figures costs $4 : 4 + 4 + 4 + 4 + 4 + 4 = $24

$$24 \div 6 = 4$$

ID1-208 Three pieces of rope are of the same length. Their total length is 15 m. How long is each piece of rope?

$$15 \div 3 = 5$$

ID1-209 Sydney arranged 18 roses in 3 bouquets. How many roses were there in each bouquet?

$$18 \div 3 = 6$$

ID1-210 Gene saves $5 a week. He wants to buy a Lego set that costs $40. How many weeks will he need to save enough money?

It will take Gene 8 weeks to save $40: 5 + 5 + 5 + 5 + 5 + 5 + 5 + 5 = $40

$$40 \div 5 = 8$$

ID1-211 Vlad, Gene, Sydney and Trenton share a prize of $20 equally. How much money did each of them receive?

Each of the 4 will receive $5: 5 + 5 + 5 + 5 = $20

$$20 \div 4 = 5$$

ID1-212 Trenton tied 32 pencils into 4 equal bundles. How many pencils were there in each bundle?

There were 8 pencils in each bundle: 8 + 8 + 8 + 8 = 32 pencils

$$32 \div 4 = 8$$

ID1-213 Sydney paid $45 for 9 flowers. What was the cost of 1 flower?

The cost of one flower is $5: 5 + 5 + 5 + 5 + 5 + 5 + 5 +5 + 5 = $45

$$45 \div 9 = 5$$

ID1-214 David arranged 70 chairs in 10 rows, each row having the same number of chairs. How many chairs were there in a row?

There are 7 chairs in each row: 7 + 7 + 7 + 7 + 7 + 7 + 7 + 7 + 7 + 7 = 70

$$70 \div 10 = 7$$

Level 2

ID2-217 Vlad has 23 candies. He wants to share some of them with Trenton, Sydney and Gene. He keeps 5 for himself and gives each of his friends the same number of candies. How many candies did each of them get?

Vlad keeps 5 candies for himself. Candies left: 23 − 5 = 18

Each of his friends will get 6 candies (6 + 6 + 6 = 18)

$$18 \div 6 = 3$$

ID2-218 Trenton has 14 pencils. He wants to arrange them in 3 equal groups. How many pencils are there in each group? Are there any pencils left over?

5 + 5 + 5 = 15 – Too much

4 + 4 + 4 = 12 - There are 4 pencils in each group

2 pencils are left over

> 14 ÷ 3 = 4 Remainder 2

ID2-219 Gene has a rope which is 32 inches long. He cuts it into pieces of 6 inches long each. How many inches of rope are left over?

6 + 6 + 6 + 6 + 6 + 2 = 32

↓ ↓ ↓ ↓ ↓

1 2 3 4 5

> 32 ÷ 6 = 5 Remainder 2

2 inches of rope are left over

ID2-220 Sydney packs 33 cookies in bags, 4 cookies in each bag. How many bags does she need?

4 + 4 + 4 + 4 + 4 + 4 + 4 + 4 + 1 = 33

↓ ↓ ↓ ↓ ↓ ↓ ↓ ↓ ↓

1 2 3 4 5 6 7 8 9

> 33 ÷ 4 = 8 Remainder 1

Sydney needs 9 bags. The last bag will only have 1 cookie.

ID2-221 If Gene gets straight A's this year, his mother promised him to double his weekly allowance to $5. What is Vlad's current allowance?

The allowance will be doubled to $5 – that means Gene gets now half of $5: $2.5

Answer: Vlad's current allowance is $2.5.

ID2-222 Vlad can solve 18 math problems in one hour. How many problems can he solve in 10 minutes?

10 minutes represent the 6th part of an hour (10 + 10 + 10 + 10 + 10 + 10 = 60).

So in order to find out how many problems can Vlad solve in 10 minutes, we need to divide 18 by 6.

We can also use the Sticky Method, explained in the Fractions Week, to find 1/6 of 18.

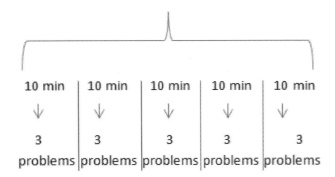

Answer: Vlad can solve 3 problems in 10 minutes.

ID2-223 Trenton has 23 candies. He wants to share some of them with 4 of his friends. He keeps 7 for himself and gives each of his friends the same number of candies. How many candies did each of them get?

Trenton keeps 7 candies for himself. Candies left: 23 − 7 = 16

Each of his 4 friends will get 4 candies (4 + 4 + 4 + 4 = 16)

$$16 \div 4 = 4$$

ID2-224 A boat can take 5 people at a time from mainland to an island near the shore. Today there are 28 people who want to go to the island. How many trips are required for the boat to take all the people to the island?

5 + 5 + 5 + 5 + 5 + 3 = 28
↓ ↓ ↓ ↓ ↓ ↓
1 2 3 4 5 6 $28 \div 5 = 5 \text{ Remainder} 3$

Level 3

ID3-226 The owner of a flower shop keeps the flowers in 4 vases. There were 7 flowers in the first vase, 4 flowers in the second vase, and 6 flowers in the third vase. The fourth vase has as many flowers as all the other three put together. The first customer buys a bouquet of 3 flowers. But then the owner wants to make more money, so he decides to sell only bouquets of 5 flowers each. After selling some bouquets, she noticed that she didn't have enough flowers to make another bouquet. How many flowers did she have left? How many customers bought flowers?

V1: 7 flowers; V2: 4 flowers; V3: 6 flowers

V4: 7 + 4 + 6 = 17 flowers

Total numbers of flowers: 17 + 17 = 34 flowers

First customer bought 3 flowers. Remaining flowers: 34 – 3 = 31 flowers

> 31 ÷ 5 = 6 Remainder 1

She had 1 flower left. There were 6 customers who bought 5 flower bouquets and 1 customer who bought a 3 flower bouquet. In total, 7 customers.

ID3-227 Vlad has 12 cookies. He eats either 2 cookie or 3 cookies a day.
Question 1: At least how many days will the cookies last?
Question 2: At most how many days will the cookies last?

At least: | 12 ÷ 3 = 4 days | At most: | 12 ÷ 2 = 6 days |

ID3-228 There are 4 chickens and some cows in the barn. The chickens and the cows have 40 legs altogether. How many cows are there in the barn?

The 4 chickens have 4 x 2 = 8 legs

The cows have the rest of the legs: 40 – 8 = 32 legs

Each cow has 4 legs, so there are 8 cows in the barn:

> 32 ÷ 4 = 8

ID3-229 There are 3 chickens and some pigs in the barn. The chickens and the pigs have 30 legs altogether. How many pigs are there in the barn?

3 chickens have 3 x 2 = 6 legs

The remaining legs are 30 – 6 = 24

Number of pigs in the farm:

> 24 ÷ 4 = 6

ID3-230 The pigs in the barn have all 32 legs. How many eyes do they have?

There are 8 pigs in the farm:

> 32 ÷ 4 = 8

They all have 16 eyes: 8 x 2 = 16 eys

ID3-231 There are 24 students in Mrs. Mustola's class. Half of them went to the Math Pentathlon competition. One third of the students who participated in the Math Pentathlon competition won medals. How many student got medals?

Half of the students go to Math Pentathlon:

$24 \div 2 = 12$

ID3-232 In Mrs. Johns' class there are 21 students. After she pairs each boy with a girl for chess games, she realizes that half of the boys don't have pairs. How many boys are in the class?

The girls are paired with some of the boys to play chess:

Girls who play chess	
Boys who play chess	

The number of boys who don't have chess partners is half of the total number of boys, so it is equal with the number of boys who play chess:

The rest of the boys	

Girls who play chess	Boys who play chess	Rest of the boys

21 students

We divide 21 by 3 to find out the number of students associated with each rectangle.

$21 \div 3 = 7$

There are 7 girls who play chess, 7 boys who play chess, and other 7 boys who don't have chess partners.

Answer: There are 14 boys in the class.

ID3-233 Daria has 24 problems to solve. She can solve either 2 problems or 3 problems a day.
Question 1: At least how many days will Daria need to solve all the problems?
Question 2: At most how many days will Daria need to solve all the problems?

Question 1. Daria will need a **minimum number (at least)** of days if she solves 3 problems a day.

```
24 ÷ 3 = 8
```

Answer 1: Daria will need at least 8 days to solve all the problems.

Question 2. Daria will need a **maximum number (at most)** of days if she solves 2 problems a day.

```
24 ÷ 2 = 12
```

Answer 2: Daria will need at most 12 days to solve all the problems.

ID3-234 There is an equal number of chickens and rabbits in a barn. The total number of legs is 36. The farmer has only 24 carrots left to feed the rabbits. If a rabbit eats 2 carrots every day, how many days will the carrots last?

At this level, it is safe to use the Trial and Error method. Anything else might confuse the students.

	Chickens	Rabbits	Total Legs	Comment
Trial 1	2	2	(2 x 2) + (2 x 4) = 12	The total number of legs is 36. Keep going.
Trial 2	3	3	(3 x 2) + (3 x 4) = 18	The total number of legs is 36. Keep going.
Trial 3	5	5	(5 x 2) + (5 x 4) = 30	The total number of legs is 36. Keep going.
Trial 4	6	6	(6 x 2) + (6 x 4) = 36	Stop. There are 6 chickens and 6 rabbits.

A rabbit eats 2 carrots a day, so 6 rabbits will eat 6 x 2 = 12 carrots every day.

The farmer has 24 carrots left, which will last 2 days: 12 + 12 = 24.

Answer: The carrots will last 2 days.

Three Little Birds

LB-235 There are 17 students in the class. Sydney did a survey and she found out that 10 students like math and 12 students like reading. How many students like both math and reading?

If we add the number of students who like math and the number of students who like reading, we get 10 + 12 = 22. But there are only 17 students in the class. So the difference is the number of students who like both math and reading:

22 − 17 = 5

Venn diagram:

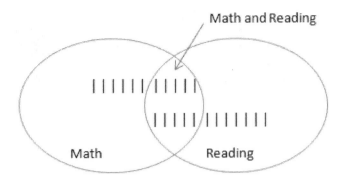

Answer: 5 students like both math and reading

LB-236 Vlad's grandma has hens and pigs in her small farm. There are 12 hens and a total of 72 legs. How many pigs does Grandma have?

12 hens have 12 x 2 = 24 legs

The pigs have the remaining legs: 72 − 24 = 48

We divide 48 by 4 to find the number of pigs: 48 / 4 = 12

Answer: Grandma has 12 pigs in her farm.

LB-237 In Mrs. Johns' class there are 22 students. After she pairs each boy with a girl for a dance recital, she will have 6 boys left out. How many boys are in the class?

Apart from the 6 boys who don't have dance partners, all the other students can form boy-girl pairs.

22 − 6 = 12 students can form boy-girl pairs. Half of them are boys – half of 12 is 6 boys.

So there are 6 boys who have dance partners and another 6 who don't.

Answer: There are 12 boys in the class.

Angry Bird

AB-238 A group of fairies went to a small village to give presents to the kids. Some of the fairies had 2 wings and some have 4 wings. There were three times as many fairies with 2 wings as fairies with 4 wings. Altogether, all the fairies had 30 wings. How many fairies went to the village?

Trial and Error:

There were three times as many fairies with 2 wings as fairies with 4 wings.

(Fairies with 2 wings) = 3 x (Fairies with 4 wings)

Number of fairies with 4 wings	Number of fairies with 2 wings	Total number of wings	Total number of fairies	Correct?
1	3	1x4 + 3x2 = 10	4	No, 10 <> 30
2	6	2x4 + 6x2 = 20	8	No, 20<> 30
3	9	3x4 + 9x2 = 30	12	Yes, 30=30

Answer: 12 fairies went to the village.

Week 8 *241, 243, 245 & 247, 249*

Level 1

NR1-239 How many numbers from 10 to 99 are there where both digits are even?

The students should know that zero is an even number (because it is divisible by 2 but that's more difficult to explain to a 2nd grader).

20, 22, 24, 26, 28,

40, 42, 44, 46, 48,

60, 62, 64, 66, 68,

80, 82, 84, 86, 88

Answer: There are 20 numbers with both digits even between 10 and 99.

NR1-240 What is the largest even number among the following numbers?

87, 11, 22, 99, 45, 48, 68, 73, 44

Even numbers: 22, 48, 68, 44

Answer: The largest even number is 68

NR1-241 The houses on my street are numbered with consecutive even numbers. The first house has the number 4 and the last one is numbered 22. How many houses are on my street?

List all the even numbers between 4 and 22:

4, 6, 8, 10, 12, 14, 16, 18, 20, 22

Count all the numbers.

Answer: There are 10 houses on my street.

NR1-242 If 9 + X = 24, how much is X + X?

We have to find X first. What do I have to add to 9 to get 24? 24 − 9 = 15

So X = 15 and X + X = 15 + 15 = 30

Answer: X + X = 30

NR1-243 If 12 + 34 = X − 20, what is X?

12 + 34 = X - 20
    46 = X -20
X = 46 + 20 = 76

Answer: X = 20

NR1-244 23 + 17 = 20 + X. Find X.

23 + 17 = 20 + X
40 = 20 + X
X = 40 + 20

NR1-245 How many rectangles are in the picture below?

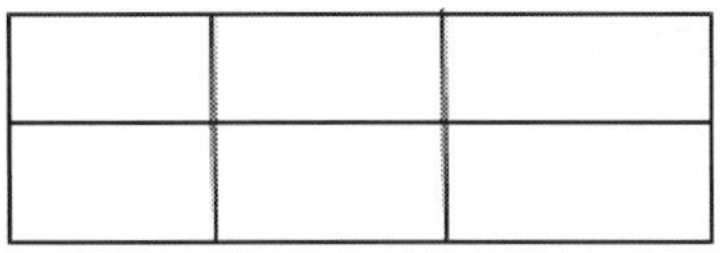

We will assign a letter to every small rectangle:

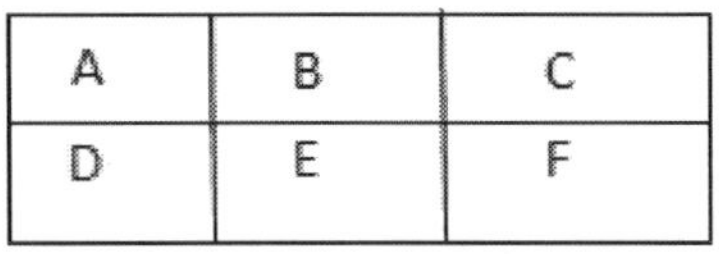

A	B	C
D	E	F

Let's count all 2 letter rectangles:
AB, DE, AD, BE, BC, EF, CF
Let's count all 3 letter rectangles:
ABC, DEF
4 letter rectangles:
ABDE, BCEF
There are no 5 letter rectangles.
6 letter rectangle:
ABCDEF
So there are 12 rectangles in the picture.

NR1-246 What is the difference between the largest odd number and the smallest even number among the following numbers?

35, 12, 17, 22, 43, 54, 63, 58, 28, 38

The largest odd number is 43
The smallest even number is 12
The difference between them is 43 − 12 = 31

NR1-247 The houses on Gene' street are numbered with consecutive odd numbers. Gene's house has the number 5 and there are 6 houses between his house and Sydney's house. What number does Sydney's house have?

5, 7, 9, 11, 13, 15, 17, 19

Answer: Sydney's house has the number 19

NR1-248 What is the largest number among the following, which has an even sum of its digits?

28, 35, 34, 45, 25, 47, 39

The largest number is 47. Check if the sum of its digits is even: 4 + 7 = 11 − No
The next largest number is 45. Check if the sum of its digits is even: 4 + 5 = 9 − No
The next largest number is 39. Check if the sum of its digits is even: 3 + 9 = 12 − Yes

Answer: 39

Level 2

NR2-249 I am an even number. I am greater than 12, but less than 24. When you count by 5s, you will find me. What number am I?

We count by 5 and write down the numbers that are between 12 and 25: 15 and 20. 20 is the only even number.

```
5    10    15   (20)    25
      ↑           ↑
      12          24
```

Answer: I am 20.

NR2-250 What is the smallest 2-digit odd number you can make by using 2 of the following numbers?

2, 4, 5, 9, 1, 3

We pick the smallest tenth digit: 1

Then we pick the smallest unit digit that is odd: 3 (we can't pick 1 because it was already used and the problem asks us to use 2 digits).

Answer: 13

NR2-251 Vlad's dad's age is an odd number. He is older than 27 and younger than Gene's dad. If you count by 5, you will find Vlad's dad's age. If Gene's dad is 38, how old is Vlad's dad?

He is older than 27 and younger than 38.

We count by 5 and write down the numbers that are between 27 and 38: 30 and 35. 35 is the only odd number:

```
5    10    15    20    25    30   (35)    40
                        ↑            ↑
                        27           38
```

Answer: Vlad's dad is 35 years old.

NR2-252 How many even numbers are there between 13 and 21 that have the sums of their digits also even?

List all the even numbers between 13 and 21:

14, 16, 18, 20

The sums of their digits are 4+1 = 5 –odd, 1 + 6 = 7 - odd, 1 + 8 = 9 - odd, 2 + 0 = 2 EVEN!

Answer: There is only one even number between 13 and 21 that has the sum of its digits also even.

Look at the following numbers: 12, 5, 14, 8, 10. What is the largest difference between 2 of these numbers? What is the smallest?

The largest difference is between the maximum and minimum number.

Max – Min = 14 – 5 = 9

The smallest difference is 2 - between 8 and 10, or between 12 and 14.

NR2-254 There are 145 students in the North Hill elementary school. 20 of them are kindergarteners, 25 first graders, 28 second graders, 30 third graders, 22 fourth graders. How many fifth graders are in the school?

The rest of the students are 5th graders:

145 − (20 + 25 + 28 + 30 + 22) = 145 − 125 = 20

Answer: There are 20 5th graders.

NR2-255 There are 6 cards in a box. The cards are numbered 1 through 6. When Gordon takes one card out of the box, the sum of the remaining ones is 16. What card did Gordon take out?

The sum of all the numbers on the cards is 1 + 2 + 3 + 4 + 5 + 6 = 21

After Gordon takes a card out, the sum of the remaining ones is 16.

So the number on the card extracted by Gordon is 21 − 16 = 5

Answer: Gordon took out the card with number 5

NR2-256 What number must be added to the sum of 15 and 8 to equal the sum of 18 and 17?

The sum of 15 and 8 is 23
The sum of 18 and 17 is 35
What number must be added to 23 to equal 35?

Answer: 35 − 23 = 12

NR2-257 Find the sum of all the numbers that are inside the ellipse and outside the square.

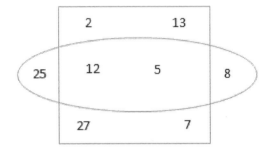

25 and 8 are the only numbers that are inside the ellipse and outside of square.

Answer: 25 + 8 = 33

NR2-258 Bobby, Frankie and Josh chose the numbers for their soccer jerseys. The numbers on the jerseys are 7, 12 and 21. Bobby's jersey has an odd number. Frankie's jersey has the largest number. What number is on Josh's jersey?

We'll start with Frankie, who has the greatest number of the jersey – that's 21.

Bobby has an odd number, and, since 21 is already taken, the only remaining odd number is 7 and belongs to Bobby.

The remaining number, 12, must belong to Josh.

Answer: Josh's jersey has number 12.

Level 3

NR3-259 The sum of Vlad's age and Trenton's age is 12. The sum of the Trenton's age and Gene's age is 15. Vlad and Trenton were born in the same year. How old is Gene?

Subjects:
V   T   G

Facts:
The sum of Vlad's age and Trenton's age is 12:
V + T = 12
The sum of the Trenton's age and Gene's age is 15:
T + G = 15
Vlad and Trenton were born in the same year
V = T
6 + 6 =12, so V = T = 6
G = 15 – T = 15 – 6 = 9
Answer: Gene is 9 years old

NR3-260 John lives in New York in a sky scraper. One day, he visited Sydney who lives on the 25th floor in the same building. John took the elevator and went up 19 floors, but then he realized that he passed Sydney's floor. He then took the elevator down 8 floors to get to Sydney's floor. On which floor does John live?

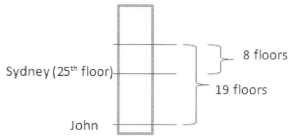

How many floors are between John's apartment and Sydney's apartment?
    19 – 8 = 11 floors
If Sydney's lives on the 25th floor and there are 11 floors between John and Sydney, what floor does John live on?
    25 – 11 = 14
Answer: John lives on the 14th floor.

NR3-261 A cat, a mouse and a squirrel weigh together 10 pounds. The cat and two mice weigh 8 pounds. The squirrel and 3 mice weigh as much as 2 cats. How much does a squirrel weigh?

With this kind of problems, the first step is to extract and code the information. The cat becomes C, the mouse becomes M, the squirrel becomes S. Then all the information is translated into number sentences, or equations. The result is a system of equations:

C + M + S = 10
C + 2M = 6

S + 3M = 2C

Now we try to combine these equations in one way or another. Add them, subtract them, and substitute one with another. We play with them until we come up with an idea. What if we add the first 2 equations together? We add the left sides and the right sides of the equations separately:

```
C + M + S = 10
C + 2M    = 6           But we also know that S + 3M = 2C
------------------                So we can replace S + 3M with 2C
2C + 3M + S = 16
```

2C + 3M + S = 16 becomes 2C + 2C = 16
4C = 16
C = 16 ÷ 4 = 4
So the **cat weighs 4 pounds**
We go back to the second equation:
C + 2M = 6, and replace C with 4:
4 + 2M = 6
2M = 2, that means M = 1. So the **mouse weighs 1 pound.**
We now replace the cat and the mouse in the first equation:
C + M + S = 10 becomes 4 + 1 + S = 10, which gives us S = 5

Answer: The squirrel weighs 5 pounds.

NR3-262 A bag of red gems weighs 10 ounces. A bag of red gems together with a bag of white gems weigh as much as 3 bags of red gems. How much do 3 bags of white gems weigh?

R = 10
R + W = 3R
10 + W = 30
W = 20   The bag of white gems weighs 20 pounds.

NR3-263 I am a number. Add me to myself, then add 12 and subtract 5. You will get 21. What number am I?

I am a number. Let's call this number Me.

Me + Me + 12 − 5 = 21

Me + Me = 21 + 5 − 12 = 14

Me = 7

Answer: I am the number 7.

NR3-264 Vlad and Gene went to soccer tryouts at the beginning of the season. They sat on the bench along with other kids waiting for their turn. There are 24 kids to the left of Vlad and other 36 kids to the left. Gene sat right in the middle of the bench, with the same number of kids sitting on his left and right side. How many kids were sitting between Gene and Vlad?

24 ⟵ Vlad ⟶ 36

How many kids were there in all?

(24 to the right of Vlad) + (Vlad) + (36 to the left of Vlad)
24 + 1 + 36 = 61
There were 61 kids in all.
Gene sat in the middle of them, so there are 30 kids to the left of him and another 30 to the right.
Vlad is the 24th on the bench, counting from left to right.
Gene is the 31st on the bench
There are 31 – 24 -1 kids between Vlad and Gene.

Answer: There are 6 kids between Vlad and Gene.

NR3-265 Vlad, Daria, and Delilah went to pick apples. Vlad picked 10 apples. Daria picked 12 apples less than Delilah. Delilah picked 3 times more apples than Vlad. How many apples did they all pick?

Vlad picked 10 apples.

Delilah picked 3 times more apples than Vlad – that means she picked 30 apples.

Daria picked 12 apples less than Delilah. So Daria picked 30 -12 = 18 apples.

All of them picked 10 + 30 + 18 = 58 apples.

Answer: 58 apples.

NR3-266 Vlad, Gene, and Sydney went to Panera Bread to buy snack. Vlad bought 1 muffin, 2 cookies, and 3 bagels, and paid $27. Gene bought 4 muffins, 2 cookies, and 3 bagels, and paid $36. Sydney bought just a muffin and a cookie for $5. How much is a cookie?

Subjects: Muffin (M), Cookie (C), Bagel (B)

Vlad: 1M + 2C + 3B = 27

Gene: 4M + 2C + 3B = 36

The only 2 things that are different in the equations above are the number of muffins and the total costs. Gene bought 3 more muffins and paid $9 more. That means a muffin costs $3.

Sydney bought a muffin and a cookie for $5. We found out above that the muffin costs $3, so the cookie costs 5 – 3 = $2.

Answer: The cookie costs $2.

NR3-267 Daria and Delilah have $36 together. Daria bought 4 cupcakes with all her money. Delilah paid twice as much for 6 muffins and she spent all her money too. How much does a muffin cost?

Delilah paid 2 times more than Daria, and together, they paid $32.

Daria: [ ]

Delilah: [ ] [ ]

Daria and Delilah: [ ] [ ] [ ]
$36

12 + 12 + 12 = 36, so one rectangle represents $12

Daria: [$12]

Delilah: [$12] [$12]

So Daria spent $12 on 4 cupcakes, and Delilah spent $24 on 6 muffins. That means a cupcake is $3 and a muffin is $4.

Answer: A muffin costs $4.

NR3-268 X is a number. If I double it, add 12 to it, and then subtract 36, I get again X. What number is X?

$2X + 12 - 36 = X$
$X + X - 24 = X$
$X = 24$

Three Little Birds

LB-269 Bobby, Frankie and Josh chose the numbers for their soccer jerseys. The numbers on the jerseys are 7, 12 and 21. Bobby's jersey has an odd number. Frankie's jersey has the largest number. What number is on Josh's jersey?

Bobby's number is odd, so it can be either 7 or 21

Frankie has the largest number – that's 21. Then Bobby's number is the other odd number – 7.

That means Josh chose the remaining number, 12.

Answer: 12

LB-270 The rectangles in the house below cost $5 dollars each and the triangles cost $10 each. How much did the front of the house cost?

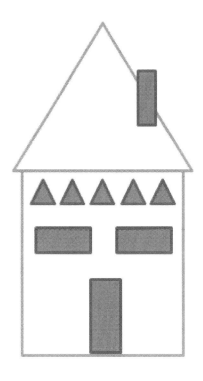

Triangles: 5 small triangles above the windows and the roof – 6 triangles in all:

5 x 6 = $30

Rectangles: 2 windows, one door, one chimney, and lower side of the house: 5 rectangles in all.

5 x 10 = $50

Total: 30 + 50 = $80

Answer: $80

LB-271 There are 6 cards in a box. The cards are numbered 1 through 6. When Trenton takes two cards out of the box, the sum of the remaining ones is 11. What cards did Trenton take out?

The sum of all 6 cards is:

1 + 2 + 3 + 4 + 5 + 6 = 21

The sum of the remaining ones is 11, so the sum of the cards taken out by Trenton is:

21 − 11 = 10

The problem is now reduced to finding two numbers from 1 to 6, which have the sum 10.

Through trial and error, we find the 2 numbers: 4 and 6.

Answer: 4 and 6.

Angry Bird

AB-272 John, Olivia and Ken are the top 3 students in a math tournament. They will all get medals: gold for 1st place, silver for 2nd place, bronze for 3rd place. John and Ken together accumulated 10 points. Ken had 4 more points than John, and Olivia had 2 less points than Ken. What medal is Olivia going to get and with what score?

Subjects: John (J), Olivia (O), Ken (K)

Facts:

Ken had 4 more points than John, and they both have 10 points combined:

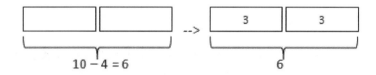

Let's see what the value of a rectangle is:

No we are going back to the first step:

(J) [3]   = 3
(K) [3][4]   = 7

So Jack has 3 points and Ken has 7 points.

Olivia has 2 points less than Ken: 7 - 2 = 5 points.

Gold: Ken with 7 points
Silver: Olivia with 5 points
Bronze: Jack with 3 points
Answer: Olivia got the silver medal with 5 points.

Rock and Roll – More Practice Problems

RR-273 One rainy day, Daria, Sydney and Delilah played a card game. There could be only one winner in that game, without any ties. If one player won, the other 2 lost. Daria lost 3 games, Sydney lost 6 games, and Delilah lost 7 games. How many games did Daria win?

Solution:

If one player wins, the other 2 lose. That means there are always 2 players who lose a game.

In total, there were 3 + 6 + 7 = 16 losses. With 2 losses per game, that means the girls played 16/2 = 8 games altogether. Daria lost 3 games and won 8 – 3 = 5 games.

Answer: Daria won 5 games.

RR-274 Vlad picked 36 apples. He gave a half of them to his friend Jacob. Then he gave a third of the remaining ones to his neighbor. But then Jacob said he had too many and he gave 4 apples back to Vlad. Finally, Vlad gave half of the apples to his brother. How many apples was Vlad left with?

Solution:

Half of 36 is 18. Vlad has now 18 apples.
One third of 18 is 6. Vlad has now 18 – 6 = 12
Jacob gave Vlad back 4 apples. Vlad has now 12 + 4 = 16
Half of 16 is 8. Vlad has now 8 apples.
Answer: Vlad was left with 8 apples.

RR-275 Sydney, Trenton and Vlad have 64 Christmas cards altogether. Vlad and Sydney have the same number of cards. Trenton and Sydney have together 49 cards. How many cards does Vlad have?

Answer: 15 (a similar problem was solved here – AB034)

RR-276 Don, John, Terry and Charley are brothers. John is 3 years younger than Terry. Charley is 5 years younger than Terry. Don is 3 years younger than John. Who is the youngest?

Solution:

```
              John  ←——— 3 years ———— Terry
       Charley ←————— 5 years ————————— Terry
Don ←— 3 years —— John ←——— 3 years ———— Terry
```

John is 3 years younger than Terry, and Don is 3 years younger than John. That means Don is 6 years younger than Terry, whereas Charley is only 5 years younger than Terry. So Don is the youngest among all the brothers.

Answer: Don is the youngest.

RR-277 John is 4 years old. Mark is 7 years older than John and Edward is 5 years younger than Mark. What will be the sum of their ages 5 years later?

Solution:

John is 4

Mark is 7 years older than John, so Mark is 4 + 7 = 11

Edward is 5 years younger than Mark, so Edward is 11 – 5 = 6

5 years later:

John will be 4 + 5 = 9

Mark will be 11 + 5 = 16

Edward will be 6 + 5 = 11

The sum of their ages will be 9 + 16 + 11 = 36

Answer: The sum of their ages will be 36 after 5 years.

RR-278 Vlad has all kinds of coins in his piggy bank – pennies, dimes, nickels, and quarters. What is the minimum number of coins that Vlad would need to pay the exact amount for a notebook that costs 49 cents? What is the maximum number?

Solution:

We start with the coins having the biggest value. Can we use 2 quarters? No, that would be 50 cents.

So we'll use only 1 quarter. We need 49 – 25 = 24 cents more.

The coin with the next biggest value is the dime – we can use 2 dimes. We would then need 24 – 20 = 4 cents more. We can only cover that with 4 pennies.

So the minimum number of coins Vlad can use is 8 – 2 quarters, 2 dimes and 4 pennies.

The maximum number of coins is 49, if Vlad will use only pennies.

RR-279 There are 3 2nd grade classes in North Hill Elementary School. There are 34 students in the first 2 classes combined. There are 8 more students in the first class than in the second, and 3 more in the third than in the second. How many students were in the third 2nd grade class?

Solution:

There are 34 students in the first 2 classes combined:

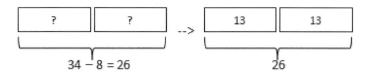

Find the value of a rectangle:

```
   ?      ?              13     13
 ─────────────    -->  ─────────────
   34 – 8 = 26              26
```

Let's go back where we started:

(1st class) | 13 | 8 | = 21
(2nd class) | 13 | | = 13

There are 3 more students in the third class than in the second class.

3rd Class : 13 + 3 = 16

Answer: There are 16 students in the third classroom.

RR-280 We are 2-digit numbers. The sum of the 2 digits is 11, and the difference is 5. What numbers are we?

Solution:

Trial and error is the best bet for 2nd graders:

Think of 2 numbers that add up to 11:

5 and 6; their difference is 1, we need 2 numbers that are further apart

2 and 9; their difference is 7, too much

3 and 8; their difference is 5 – bingo!

Answer: We are numbers 3 and 8.

RR-281 Vlad was born in 2005. His mom was 27 years old when he was born. Vlad's sister, Daria, was 4 years old at that time. In what year was his mom born?

Solution:

This is a problem that provides too much information to confuse the students. We really don't need any information about Vlad's sister here.

If Vlad's mom was 27 in 2005, that means she was born in 2005 – 27 = 1978

RR-282 Gene builds a Lego house with 34 red and yellow pieces of Lego. There are 6 more yellow pieces than red pieces. How many red pieces does Gene have? How many yellow?

Solution:

RR-283 Daria arranged her collection of marbles in small boxes. She likes patterns, so she put 1 marble in the first box, 2 in the second, 3 in the third and so on. Her collection numbers 36 marbles. How many boxed did she need?

Solution:

1 + 2 = 3

1 + 2 + 3 = 6

1 + 2 + 3 + 4 = 10

1 + 2 + 3 + 4 + 5 = 15

1 + 2 + 3 + 4 + 5 + 6 = 21

1 + 2 + 3 + 4 + 5 + 6 + 7 = 28

1 + 2 + 3 + 4 + 5 + 6 + 7 + 8 = 36 STOP

Answer: Daria will need 8 boxes for her collection of 36 marbles.

RR-284 Vlad is 5 years older than Daria. The sum of their ages is 19. How old is Daria?

Solution:

Vlad is 5 years older than Daria:

The sum of their ages is 19:

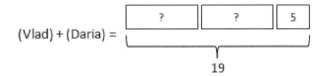

Find what the "?" is:

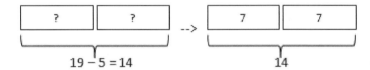

We then go back where we started:

(Vlad) [7][5] = 12

(Daria) [7] = 7

Answer: Daria is 7 years old.

RR-285 Vlad and Daria went to OfficeMax to buy pencils. Vlad bought 2 blue pencils for 13 cents each. Daria saw some red pencils that were sold by the pair – 7 cents each pair. She liked them and bought 8. Who paid more for the pencils? How much more?

Solution:

Daria bought 8 pencils – that is 4 pairs. She paid 7 cents for each pair: 7 x 4 = 28 cents

Vlad bought 2 pencils for 13 cents each – that is 2 x 13 = 26 cents

Answer: Daria paid more for the pencils. She paid 28 – 26 = 2 cents more.

RR-286 Vlad has 6 more pencils than Gene. Sydney has as many pencils as Vlad and Gene have together. If Vlad has 13 pencils, how many pencils does Sydney have?

Solution:

Vlad has 13 pencils. He has 6 more pencils than Gene. So Gene has 13 – 6 = 7 pencils.

Sydney has as many pencils as Vlad and Gene together. She has 13 + 7 = 20 pencils.

Answer: Sydney has 20 pencils.

RR-287 Vlad, Sydney, Trenton and Gene wanted to share 3 big cookies so they each had the same amount. Is it possible? If yes, what fraction did each person receive?

Solution:

Divide each cookie in 4 parts. Each of them will take one part (1/4) from each every cookie.

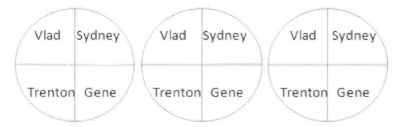

And since there are 3 cookies, that means each of them will take 3/4 of the cookie.

Answer: Yes, it is possible. Each of them will take 3/4.

RR-288 Vlad bought a total of 12 red and green t-shirts. He bought twice as many green t-shirts as red t-shirts. How many red t-shirts did he buy?

Solution:

Red t-shirts: ☐

Green t-shirts (twice as many): ☐ ☐

There are 12 red and green t-shirts in total:

☐ ☐ ☐
⎵
12

Each of the rectangles represents 1/3 of 12, which is 4.

So there are 4 red t-shirts and 4+4=8 green t-shirts.

Answer: Vlad bought 4 red t-shirts.

RR-289 22 kids showed up at Vlad's birthday party. He had 3 dozens of cookies and wanted to offer each kid 2 cookies. How many more cookies did he need?

Solution:

Vlad wants to offer 2 cookies to each of the 22 kids. That means he needs 22 + 22 = 44 cookies.

He already has 3 dozens – that is 12 + 12 + 12 = 36 cookies.

He needs 44 − 36 = 8 more cookies.

Answer: He needs 8 more cookies.

RR-290 John paid for 5 pencils with 4 quarters, 4 dimes, 2 nickels. The following day he needed to buy 10 more pencils for his friend. He only had 3 quarters and 3 dimes. How much more did he need?

Solution:

4 quarters, 4 dimes, 2 nickels = 4x25 + 4x10 + 2x5 = $1.50

So Vlad paid $1.50 for 5 pencils. He would need twice more for 10 pencils – that is 1.50 + 1.50 = $3

The following day he only had 3 quarters and 3 dimes – that is $1.05

He needed 3 – 1.05 = $1.95 more to buy the 10 pencils.

Answer: He needed $1.95 more.

RR-291 Trenton and Gene collect postage stamps. Trenton has 21 stamps and gave Gene 6 stamps to have both the same number. How many did Gene have initially?

Solution:

Trenton has 21 stamps and gave Gene 6 stamps - now Trenton has 21 – 6 = 15 stamps and Gene has the same.

Initially, Gene had 15 – 6 = 9

Answer: Gene had 9 stamps initially.

RR-292 John has 3 pencils, Eric has 3 more pencils than Mark, and Mark has 3 times more pencils than John. How many pencils do they have altogether?

Solution:

John has 3 pencils.

Mark has 3 times more pencils than John – that is 3 x 3 = 3 + 3 + 3 = 9 pencils

Eric has 3 more pencils than Mark – that is 9 + 3 = 12 pencils

Answer: Together they have 3 + 9 + 12 = 24 pencils

RR-293 The concert had three 40 minutes parts with two equal breaks between the parts. The concert started at 10:20 PM and it finished at 1 AM. How long were the breaks?

Solution:

Calculate time is between 10:20 AM and 1:00 AM – 2 hours and 40 minutes.

Subtract the duration of first part: 2 hours and 40 minutes – 40 minutes = 2 hours

Subtract the duration of the second part: 2 hours – 40 minutes = 1 hour and 20 minutes

Subtract the duration of the third part: 1 hour and 20 minutes – 40 minutes = 40 minutes

So the duration of the both breaks was 40 minutes. One break was 20 minutes long.

Answer: The breaks were each 20 minutes long.

RR-294 Vlad bought 4 watermelons and 9 oranges for $36. He paid the same the same amount of money for watermelons as he paid for oranges. He also wanted to buy mangos, but one mango was $2 more expensive than one orange, so he gave up the idea. How much did a mango cost?

Solution:

Vlad paid the same amount for watermelons and oranges. So he paid one half of $36 for watermelons and the other half for oranges.
4 watermelons cost $18 – we are not interested to find the cost of one watermelon
9 oranges cost $18 – so one orange was 18/9 = $2
The mango was $2 more expensive than the orange – that means the mango was $3
Answer: The mango cost $3.

RR-295 Trenton paid $21 for 3 notebooks and 3 pencils. Gene paid $11 for 1 notebook and 3 pencils. They also bought 4 erasers. One eraser was $1 cheaper than one pencil. How much did they pay for the erasers?

Solution:

Identify the subjects: Notebooks (N), Pencils (P), Erasers (E)

Sketch the facts:

Trenton paid $21 for 3 notebooks and 3 pencils

3N + 3P = 21

Gene paid $11 for 1 notebook and 3 pencils

1N + 3P = 11

The 2 equations are similar. The difference is given by the number of notebooks and total costs. Let's write the first number sentence using the second one:

2N + 1N + 3P = 21
But
1N + 3P = 11
=> 2N + 11 = 21 => 2N = 10 => N = 5

So a notebook costs $5. We now use the second number sentence to find P:

5 + 3P = 11 => 3P = 6 => P = 2

A pencil costs $2.

The eraser costs $1 less than the pencil, so it costs 2 -1 = $1

Answer: They paid 4 x 1 = $4 for 4 erasers.

RR-296 John has a box full of chips with numbers on them. A chip can only have one of the following 3 numbers: 9, 4, 7. John extracts 3 chips and calculates the sum of the numbers written on them. The sum is less than 16 and greater than 12. He then arranges the 3 numbers in ascending order and calculates the sum between the median and the modal. What is the sum that John came up with?

Solution:

The sum is greater than 12 and less than 16, so it can be 13, 14, or 15. Use trial and error to find the numbers:
4 + 4 + 4 = 12 We need more
4 + 4 + 7 = 15 This is good. There is no other valid combination.
4 + 4 + 9 = 17 – Too much
So we found the numbers: 4, 4, 7
The median is 4 and the modal is also 4 (see Week 5 if you want to remember how the median and modal are calculated).
Answer: The sum between median and modal is 4 + 4 = 8

RR-297 Sydney brings 13 marbles, Vlad brings 11 marbles, Trenton brings 8 marbles, and Gene doesn't bring any. They put all the marbles together and divide them equally among themselves. Then Gene takes his share of marbles and gives half of them to his brother, Min. Min plays soccer in a 7-player team. He wants to give one marble to each of his team mates. How many more marbles would he need?

Solution:
They all have 13+11+8=32 marbles. They divide them equally among themselves. So each of them will have 32/4 = 8 marbles.
Gene gives half of his marbles to Min. So Min has 4 marbles. He plays soccer in a 7-player team, so he has 6 team mates, but he has only 4 marbles.
Answer: Min needs 6-4 = 2 more marbles for his team mates.

RR-298 Chris was born on June 17th, 2005. Dora was born on Sep 23rd, 2006. John was born on Aug 16th, 2007. Mark was born on Oct 24th, 2007. They decide to get all together on Sep 1st 2013 and have a party. What will be the sum of their ages?

Solution:

What age will each of them have on Sep 1st, 2013?

Chris was born on June 17th, 2005 – he will be 2013 – 2005 = 8

Dora was born on Sep 23rd, 2006 – she will be **2012** – 2006 = 6 (her birthday is after Sep 1st)

John was born on Aug 16th, 2007 – he will be 2013 – 2007 = 6

Mark was born on Oct 24th, 2007 – he will be **2012** – 2007 = 5 (his birthday is after Sep 1st)

Answer: The sum of their ages on Sep 1st 2013 will be 8 + 6 + 6 + 5 = 25.

RR-299 The shelter next to Vlad's house has a number of dogs. The difference between their legs and their tails is 27. Every week 2 new dogs are brought to the shelter and 5 dogs are adopted by new families. In how many weeks will the shelter get empty?

Solution:

If there were 1 dog in the shelter, the difference between the his legs and his tails would have been 4 -1 = 3

2 dogs -> 4 + 4 – 1 – 1 = 6

3 dogs -> 4 + 4 + 4 - 1 – 1 - 1 = 9

We can now see the pattern:

4 dogs -> 12

5 dogs -> 15

6 dogs -> 18

7 dogs -> 21

8 dogs -> 24

9 dogs -> 27 STOP

So there are 9 dogs in the shelter.

Every week 2 new dogs are brought to the shelter and 5 dogs leave.

Week 1: 9 + 2 – 5 = 6

Week 2: 6 + 2 – 5 = 3

Week 3: 3 + 2 – 5 = 0 STOP

Answer: The shelter will get empty after 3 weeks.

RR-300 The distance between city A and city B is 123 miles. The distance between city B and city C is 88 miles. We don't have any information about where these 3 cities are located. What is the minimum distance between A and C? What is the maximum?

Solution:

The distance between A and C is minimum when they are as close as possible. That would be when C is located on the straight line between A and B:

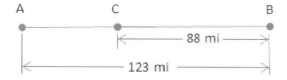

The distance in this case would be 123 – 88 = 35 mi.

The distance between A and C is maximum when they are the farthest apart. That would be when B is located on the straight line between A and C:

The distance in this case would be 123 + 88 = 211 mi.

Answer: The minimum distance is 35 mi. The maximum distance is 211 mi.

Made in the USA
Lexington, KY
02 February 2015